JELLY SHOTS

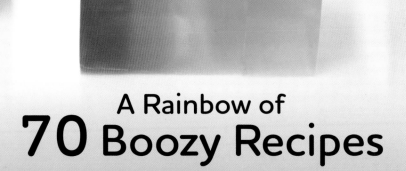

A Rainbow of
70 Boozy Recipes

Michelle Cordero

Race Point
PUBLISHING

Race Point Publishing
An imprint of Quarto Publishing Group USA Inc.
142 West 36th Street, 4th Floor
New York, NY 10018

RACE POINT PUBLISHING and the distinctive Race Point Publishing logo are trademarks of Quarto Publishing Group USA, Inc.

Editorial Directors: Jeannine Dillon and Hallie Einhorn
Managing Editor: Erin Canning
Design: Heidi North
Photography: Glenn Scott
Food Styling: Natasha St. Hailare Taylor

ISBN: 978-1-63106-025-0

Library of Congress Cataloging-in-Publication Data is available

Printed in China

1 3 5 7 9 10 8 6 4 2

www.racepointpub.com

CONTENTS

Dear Party People,

Jelly shots have come a long way since the days of a Dixie cup filled with vodka and cherry-flavored gelatin. Today, jelly shots are glammed up, creative, bite-sized cocktails that you can serve for every occasion. They are usually the first things to disappear at a party, and even better, they're easy to make.

In this cookbook and on my blog, I pride myself on making creative and fun jelly shots that everyone can make with things you may already have in your kitchen or can buy at the grocery store. I don't use hard-to-find ingredients or fancy molds that you have to order online, and I try to keep each recipe down to one bottle of booze so you aren't spending a fortune.

On any given weekend, you might find me with a vodka-soaked gummy bear stuck in my hair after a photo shoot. My husband brings leftover jelly shots to work (who does that?). I have fifty boxes of flavored gelatin in my pantry at all times, and we have an ongoing competition about who can come up with the craziest jelly shot idea that I can turn into a recipe.

Why do I do all this? Because who doesn't want to be that person who brings the one thing to the party that everyone talks about? This cookbook has seventy jelly shot recipes that will be the hit of the party. I promise.

Cheers to you and all the accolades you're going to receive from these recipes!

Michelle, a.k.a. the Jelly Shot Queen

GETTING STARTED

I pride myself on creating easy recipes that anyone can follow, and I make each one with ingredients and tools you may already have on hand or that can be found at your local grocery store or, in some cases, a craft or party store.

Basic Tools and Ingredients

- **Knox gelatin:** setting agent for shots. It is usually sold—4 packets per box (¼ ounce, or 7 g, per packet)—next to the pudding and boxed flavored gelatin in grocery stores.
- **Melon baller:** for scooping fruit from oranges, lemons, limes, strawberries, or peaches.
- **Mini cookie or fondant cutters (shapes: square, heart, triangle, round, gingerbread man, and Christmas tree):** for cutting out shots. It's important that these are mini sized, so I find that fondant cutters work best. They can be found in the baking section of a craft store. You can also cut out shapes with a knife.
- **Mini rubber spatula:** for carefully removing shots from pan after they set.
- **Molds (optional):** for shaping shots. Note: In a few recipes I use a bite-sized brownie silicone mold that you can buy in the baking section of most craft stores but a 9 x 13-inch (23 x 33 cm) pan works just as well, as long as you cut them out carefully and uniformly. I used a bunny-shaped silicone mold for the Marshmallow Bunnies shots (page 35) and a mini donut pan for the Pink Frosted Donut shots (page 132). Both can be found in the baking section of a craft store.
- **Nonstick cooking spray:** for lightly greasing pans when making shots.
- **Pans (9 x 13 inch, or 23 x 33 cm; 9 x 9 inch, or 23 x 23 cm, square cake; and 7½ x 3½ inch, or 19 x 9 cm, loaf):** for making shots.
- **2-ounce (60 mL) clear plastic shot glasses:** for serving shots. These can be found at your local party store or in some grocery stores.

Frequently Asked Questions

When making anything, including jelly shots, the process can lead to some trial and error. Here I have included some FAQs you may have while preparing your jelly shots.

Q: **What do I do with the leftover gelatin after I cut out my shots?**

A: When cutting out shapes for shots with cookie or fondant cutters, you will inevitably have some leftover gelatin, especially when using a in 9 x 13-inch (23 x 33 cm) pan. If you don't want to toss it, do your best to make uniform shapes with what is left and serve the shapes after your guests have finished the first round of shots.

Q: **How do I cut shapes if I don't have mini cookie or fondant cutters?**

A: The best way to get multiple uniform shots is to run a rubber spatula along the sides of your 9 x 13-inch (23 x 33 cm) pan to loosen the gelatin. Don't try to flip out the entire pan in one piece. Cut it in four strips across the width of the pan and carefully lift out each piece with your rubber spatula and then slide your hand underneath. Place each strip on a cutting board and slice into uniform cubes. If you need a circular shape you can use the rim of a shot glass to cut out each shape. You can also cut free-form shapes with a knife.

Q: **What if I don't want to use alcohol in my shots?**

A: Simply replace each cup (240 mL) of alcohol with a cup (240 mL) of water or juice of your choice.

Q: **Why do you use Thai coconut milk? Can I use regular milk?**

A: After testing, I realized that Thai coconut milk doesn't separate, unlike Spanish coconut milk, when it's heated. It is also lactose free, super rich and creamy, and tastes great. Just make sure to stir it before use. You can also use regular milk or cream.

Q: **What is the best type of citrus fruit to make jelly shots with?**

A: I like to use the rinds of lemons or oranges to make shots. Oranges hold the most liquid and lemons hold their shape best. Limes are small and sometimes the rind can lend a bitter flavor to the gelatin, intensifying the taste of the alcohol.

Q: **Why did my layered shots separate?**

A: When you are layering your shots, for different colors, or to place a maraschino cherry or strawberry in the middle, it is important that the mixture for the top layer comes to room temperature before pouring it on the layer in the pan. Also, the bottom layer should only be refrigerated for 30–60 minutes, or until sticky and slightly set but not firm. If it's totally firm, the upper layer won't adhere as well. Check it frequently.

Q: **My shots didn't get firm enough. Why?**

A: Always refrigerate your shots for at least 2 hours. If you refrigerated them for the appropriate amount of time, double-check if you have used the right amount of Knox gelatin. Even when you use a box of flavored Jell-O, you may need to add one packet of Knox gelatin. If your shots are too firm, you may have added too much gelatin, which can also make shots grainy and give them an unpleasant texture. The rule of thumb is that for every cup (240 mL) of liquid you should add 1 packet of Knox gelatin.

Q: **When using a cookie or fondant cutter, how do I keep the shot in one piece when removing from the pan?**

A: Push once lightly with the cutter and wait, then slowly ease into the gelatin until you hit the bottom of the pan. Too much pressure may split the shot. Carefully lift with the mini rubber spatula and plate.

Q: **When filling fruit rinds, marshmallows, shot glasses, etc. with the gelatin mixture, how much should I fill them?**

A: Always fill to the top and reserve any leftover mixture you may have. Gelatin shrinks as it firms up, so you can use the leftover mixture to top the shots off as they are hardening. Make sure to set any leftover mixture in a somewhat warm spot so that it does not harden in the meantime.

Valentine's Day

PINK CHAMPAGNE

CHOCOLATE-COVERED CHERRIES

RED & WHITE WITH HEARTS

SALTED CARAMELS

WHITE CHOCOLATE WITH RASPBERRIES

St. Patrick's Day

SHAMROCKS

SHAMROCK PUDDING

PINK CHAMPAGNE

These shots are perfect for any Valentine's Day celebration or even a bridal shower or wedding. The adorable pink hearts are made with champagne and sweet almond-flavored Amaretto.

 Makes 24–30 shots

Ingredients

3 cups (715 mL) pink champagne, divided

4 x ¼-ounce (7 g) packet Knox gelatin

¼ cup (50 g) sugar

1 cup (240 mL) Amaretto

Drop of pink or red food coloring

Instructions

1. Pour 2 cups (475 mL) pink champagne in a medium saucepan. Sprinkle in gelatin and let it sit for 1 minute, letting the gelatin activate. Place saucepan over medium heat, whisking until gelatin dissolves.

2. Add the sugar and whisk until it dissolves. Bring to a light simmer, then remove from heat.

3. In a separate bowl, mix the Amaretto and the remaining 1 cup (240 mL) pink champagne. Add the pink or red food coloring to keep the pretty pink champagne color. Stir in the warm champagne mixture.

4. Pour into a lightly greased 9 x 13-inch (23 x 33 cm) pan. Refrigerate for 2 hours, or until firm.

5. Carefully cut out shots with a mini heart-shaped cookie or fondant cutter and remove from pan. Refrigerate until serving.

CHOCOLATE-COVERED CHERRIES

Inspired by chocolate-covered cherries, these little babies are easy to pick up and enjoy. They're a decadent, boozy burst of goodness.

 Makes 20–24 shots

Ingredients

2 cups (475 mL) water

6 tablespoons (168 g) hot chocolate mix

4 x ¼-ounce (7 g) packet Knox gelatin

2 cups (475 mL) cherry-, chocolate-, or whipped cream–flavored vodka

20–24 maraschino cherries with stems, halved horizontally

Instructions

1. Add water and hot chocolate to a medium saucepan and whisk until combined. Sprinkle in gelatin and let it sit for 1 minute, letting the gelatin activate. Place saucepan over medium heat, whisking until gelatin dissolves. Bring to a light simmer, then remove from heat. Add the vodka.

2. Pour half of the hot chocolate mixture into a lightly greased 9 x 13-inch (23 x 33 cm) pan. Refrigerate for 30–60 minutes, or until sticky and slightly set but not firm. Set aside remaining mixture and let come to room temperature.

3. Pour remaining hot chocolate mixture on top of layer in pan.

4. Place cherry halves with stems in rows—with enough space to cut hearts around them—in the mixture. Place pan back in the refrigerator for 2 hours, or until firm.

5. Carefully cut out shots around the cherries with a mini heart-shaped cookie or fondant cutter and remove from pan. Refrigerate until serving.

RED & WHITE HEARTS

The first time I used maraschino cherries in a shot recipe was for these heart-shaped shots. They came out exactly how I imagined them in my head. That doesn't happen often, in life or in the kitchen. I heart them.

 Makes 20–24 shots

Ingredients

½ cup (120 mL) Thai coconut milk

1½ cups (360 mL) water, divided

2 x ¼-ounce (7 g) packet Knox gelatin, divided

¼ cup (50 g) sugar

2 cups (480 mL) cherry-flavored vodka, divided

20–24 maraschino cherries with stems, halved horizontally

3-ounce (85 g) box cherry Jell-O

Instructions

1. To make the white layer, add Thai coconut milk and ½ cup (120 mL) water to a medium saucepan and whisk until combined. Sprinkle in 1 packet gelatin and let it sit for 1 minute, letting the gelatin activate. Place saucepan over medium heat, whisking until gelatin dissolves.

2. Add the sugar and whisk until it dissolves. Bring to a light simmer, then remove from heat. Add 1 cup (240 mL) vodka.

3. Pour mixture into a lightly greased 9 x 13-inch (23 x 33 cm) pan. Refrigerate for 30–60 minutes, or until sticky and slightly set but not firm.

4. Place cherry halves with stems in rows—with enough space to cut hearts around them—on the white layer.

5. To make the red layer, add 1 cup (240 mL) water and cherry Jell-O to a medium saucepan and whisk until powder dissolves. Sprinkle in 1 packet gelatin and let it sit for 1 minute, letting the gelatin activate. Place saucepan over medium heat, whisking until gelatin dissolves. Bring to a light simmer, then remove from heat. Add remaining 1 cup (240 mL) vodka. Let mixture come to room temperature.

6. Carefully pour mixture on top of the white layer so that just the tops of the cherries are visible. Refrigerate for 2 hours, or until firm.

7. Carefully cut out shots around the cherries with a mini heart-shaped cookie or fondant cutter and remove from pan. Refrigerate until serving.

SALTED CARAMELS

These shots are ev-er-y-thing—sweet, salty, creamy, and boozy. I've included instructions for making shots and bites. The bites look exactly like caramel candy squares! For a stronger caramel flavor, replace the butterscotch schnapps with caramel-flavored vodka.

 Makes 12 shots or 32–40 bites

Ingredients

½ cup (120 mL) water

1 tablespoon (28 g) caramel-flavored hot chocolate

½ cup (120 mL) evaporated milk

¼-ounce (7 g) packet Knox gelatin

¼ cup (50 g) sugar

Yellow food coloring

1 teaspoon (5 mL) coarse sea salt, plus additional for topping

½ cup (120 mL) butterscotch schnapps or caramel-flavored vodka

Instructions

1. Add water and hot chocolate to a medium saucepan and whisk until combined. Add evaporated milk and whisk again. Sprinkle in gelatin and let it sit for 1 minute, letting the gelatin activate. Place saucepan over medium heat, whisking until gelatin dissolves.

2. Add the sugar and whisk until it dissolves. Bring to a light simmer, then remove from heat.

3. Add food coloring until the mixture becomes a caramel color (I use 2–3 drops). Add 1 teaspoon (5 mL) sea salt. Add the schnapps or vodka.

4. To make shots, pour mixture in shot glasses. Refrigerate for 2 hours, or until firm. Refrigerate until serving. Top each shot with a pinch of sea salt before serving. (The salt will melt if you put it on top of each bite too soon).

5. To make bites, pour mixture into a lightly greased 7½ x 3½-inch (19 x 9 cm) loaf pan. Refrigerate for 2 hours, or until firm. Using a rubber spatula or butter knife, run it along the edge of the loaf pan to loosen the gelatin. Flip the pan onto a cutting board, releasing the gelatin whole. Slice gelatin as if you were slicing bread, into 8 slices.

6. Make 4–5 verticle slices to cut squares. Refrigerate until serving. Top each bite with a pinch of the remaining sea salt before serving. (The salt will melt if you put it on top of each bite too soon).

WHITE CHOCOLATE WITH RASPBERRIES

These shots are creamy and white chocolaty but still light, with the right amount of booze to let you know they mean business. They are almost like a boozy panna cotta. I top them with a raspberry for extra flavor and color, but you could also serve them with strawberries or blackberries.

 Makes 12 shots

Ingredients

½ cup (120 mL) water

1 tablespoon (28 g) white hot cocoa mix

½ cup (120 mL) evaporated milk

¼-ounce (7 g) packet Knox gelatin

¼ cup (50 g) sugar

½ cup (120 mL) whipped cream–flavored vodka or alcohol of choice, chilled

12 raspberries, for topping

Instructions

1. Add water and white hot chocolate to a medium saucepan and whisk until combined. Add the evaporated milk and whisk again. Sprinkle in gelatin and let it sit for 1 minute, letting the gelatin activate. Place saucepan over medium heat, whisking until gelatin dissolves.

2. Add the sugar and whisk until it dissolves. Bring to a light simmer, then remove from heat. Add the vodka. Pour the mixture into shot glasses. Refrigerate for 2 hours, or until firm.

3. Refrigerate until serving. Top each shot with a raspberry before serving.

SHAMROCKS

Rather than using a mini shamrock-shaped cookie cutter to create shamrock shapes, I prefer the simplicity of placing heart shapes together to form a clover. These are easy to make and fun for guests to eat leaf by leaf.

 Makes 24 hearts or 8 shamrocks

Ingredients

2 cups (475 mL) water

2 x (3-ounce) box green Jell-O

2 x ¼-ounce (7 g) packet Knox gelatin

2 cups (475 mL) vodka

Rainbow gummy strips

Instructions

1. Add water and green Jell-O to a medium saucepan and whisk until powder dissolves. Sprinkle in gelatin and let it sit for 1 minute, letting the gelatin activate. Place saucepan over medium heat, whisking until gelatin dissolves. Bring to a light simmer, then remove from heat. Add the vodka.

2. Pour mixture into a lightly greased 9 x 13-inch (23 x 33 cm) pan. Refrigerate for 2 hours, or until firm.

3. Carefully cut out shots with a mini heart-shaped cookie or fondant cutter. Arrange the hearts to form clovers. Slice green gummy worms or licorice to make the stems. Refrigerate until serving.

SHAMROCK PUDDING

I use pistachio instant pudding in these pudding shots because it's green and tasty and super easy to find in any grocery store. When I made these shots last minute for a party, I didn't have time to look for mini spoons, so I used cookies instead. Simply stick a cookie in your shot glass and scoop out the shot bite by bite.

 Makes 12–14 shots

Ingredients

3.4-ounce (96 g) box Jell-O pistachio instant pudding

¾ cup (180 mL) milk

½ cup (120 mL) Baileys Irish Cream

¼ cup (60 mL) Jameson Irish Whiskey

8-ounce (226 g) container extra creamy Cool Whip, thawed in refrigerator

Green food coloring (optional)

Whipped cream, for topping

Sprinkles, for topping

Package of cookies of choice

Instructions

1. Combine pudding and milk in a large bowl with an electric mixer—it will look semi-thick.

2. Fold the Irish cream, whiskey, and Cool Whip into the pudding mixture until combined—don't overmix, but there should be no lumps. If you don't think the mixture is green enough, add a couple drops of green food coloring.

3. Cover and place in freezer for 1 hour, or until firm but not frozen.

4. Spoon or pipe the pudding mixture into shot glasses. Refrigerate until serving. Top with whipped cream and sprinkles and place a sugar cookie in each shot glass to use as a spoon before serving.

Spring

CUCUMBER MINT JULEPS

MARSHMALLOWS

MINT JULEP PUDDING

MARSHMALLOW BUNNIES

Cinco de Mayo

FLAN

TEQUILA SUNRISES

STRAWBERRY MARGARITAS

JALAPEÑO MARGARITAS

CUCUMBER MINT JULEPS

A twist on a classic mint julep, these shots are refreshing and sweet, and you can eat them in one bite. For something a little different, replace the bourbon with Southern Comfort and the mint with cilantro. Also, if you are bringing these out in the heat, be sure to keep them in a cooler or the shots will melt quickly.

✳ Makes about 36–48 shots

Ingredients

10 mini cucumbers

1 cup (240 mL) water

1 cup (200 g) sugar

2 x ¼-ounce (7 g) packet Knox gelatin

1 cup (96 g) mint, muddled, divided

1 cup (240 mL) bourbon

Instructions

1. Slice mini cucumbers into 1-inch-wide (2.5 cm) segments (the larger part of the cucumber is best). Hollow each piece out with a melon baller or paring knife. Be careful not to hollow out too much or your gelatin will seep through.

2. Combine water and sugar in a medium saucepan and whisk until combined. Sprinkle in gelatin and let it sit for 1 minute, letting the gelatin activate. Place saucepan over medium heat, whisking until gelatin dissolves. Bring to a light simmer, then remove from heat.

3. Add ½ cup (48 g) muddled mint leaves to the sugar water. Add the bourbon.

4. Pour mixture into a spouted bowl or measuring cup, then carefully pour it into the hollowed-out cucumbers. Refrigerate for 2 hours, or until firm. Save any leftover mixture in case you need to top off shots as they set. Refrigerate until serving.

MARSHMALLOWS

Sometimes my husband comes up with the craziest ideas, like hollowing out a large marshmallow and filling it with alcoholic Jell-O! I didn't think it would work—I thought the gelatin would soak through the marshmallow and leak out—but I promised him that I would try it. Guess what? It works and it's so much fun to eat!

✳ Makes 24–30 shots

Ingredients

28-ounce (793 g) bag large marshmallows

¾ cup (180 mL) water

3-ounce (85 g) box Jell-O, color/flavor of choice

1 cup (240 mL) whipped cream–flavored vodka or vodka flavor of choice

Instructions

1. Use a melon baller to hollow out or clean fingers to pinch out the centers of the marshmallows. Let marshmallows sit for 1–2 hours to harden.

2. Pour water into a medium saucepan, bring to a boil, and lower heat to medium. Add the Jell-O and whisk until powder dissolves. Remove from heat. Add the vodka.

3. This step is really important. Let the mixture cool. It should be at least room temperature before you pour it into the marshmallows. If it's hot, it will melt the marshmallow and it won't work.

4. Pour mixture into a spouted bowl or measuring cup, then carefully pour it into the hardened, hollowed-out marshmallows. Save any leftover mixture in case you need to top off shots as they set. Refrigerate for 2 hours, or until firm. Refrigerate until serving.

MINT JULEP PUDDING

Big hats, Lilly Pulitzer dresses, roses, horses, and, of course, mint juleps! When it's Kentucky Derby time, you have to bring these to a party. If you want to save yourself some money and not buy two bottles of booze, you can skip the crème de menthe and add 1½ cups (350 mL) milk, ½ cup (120 mL) bourbon and a ¹⁄₁₀-ounce (3 g) packet of Duncan Hines Frosting Creations in mint chocolate. You can find it next to the frosting in the baking aisle of most grocery stores. It gives the mint flavor and color.

 Makes 24 shots

Ingredients

3.4-ounce (96 g) box Jell-O instant vanilla or white chocolate pudding

1 cup (240 mL) milk

½ cup (120 mL) bourbon

½ cup (120 mL) crème de menthe

8-ounce (226 g) container Cool Whip, thawed in refrigerator

Handful fresh mint, chopped, plus additional sprigs for garnish

Whipped cream, for topping

Instructions

1. Combine pudding and milk in a large bowl with an electric mixer—it will look semi-thick.

2. Fold the bourbon, crème de menthe, and Cool Whip into the pudding mixture until combined—don't overmix, but there should be no lumps.

3. Cover and place in freezer for 1 hour, or until firm but not frozen.

4. Fold in the chopped mint. Spoon or pipe the pudding mixture into shot glasses. Refrigerate until serving. Top with whipped cream and garnish with mint sprigs before serving.

MARSHMALLOW BUNNIES

Peeps are a staple of springtime. Once you see them on store shelves, you know warm weather is on its way. This grown-up version is adorable and easy to make. I used a bunny silicone mold for these but you could also use a square pan and a bunny-shaped cookie or fondant cutter.

 Makes 24 shots

Ingredients

1 cup (240 mL) water

¼ cup (60 mL) sweetened condensed milk

2 x ¼-ounce (7 g) packet Knox gelatin

Wilton gel food coloring in rose and lemon yellow

1 cup (240 mL) marshmallow-flavored vodka

Nonpareil or chocolate sprinkles, for topping

Instructions

1. Combine water and sweetened condensed milk in a bowl and whisk until combined. Pour the mixture into a measuring cup to equal 1 cup (240 mL) liquid. Discard any extra liquid.

2. Pour the mixture into a medium saucepan. Sprinkle in gelatin and let it sit for 1 minute, letting the gelatin activate. Place saucepan over medium heat, whisking until gelatin dissolves.

3. Add a small amount of food coloring to the mixture (I use an amount that just fills the tip of a small spoon—a little goes a long way). When mixture is desired color, bring to a light simmer. Remove from heat and add the vodka.

4. Pour mixture into a lightly greased mold or pan. Refrigerate for 2 hours, or until firm.

5. If using a mold, carefully pop the bunnies out of the mold. If using a pan, carefully cut out shots with a bunny-shaped cookie or fondant cutter and remove from pan. Refrigerate until serving. Top with sprinkles for eyes before serving.

FLAN

Flan is one of my favorite desserts. It's creamy and sweet like caramel. How can it get any better than that? Add booze! I like to make this recipe with caramel-flavored vodka, but any dark rum would complement the flan flavor as well.

 Makes 12 shots

Ingredients

3-ounce (85 g) box Jell-O instant flan with caramel sauce

1 cup (240 mL) milk

2 x ¼-ounce (7 g) packet Knox gelatin

1 cup (240 mL) caramel-flavored vodka or dark rum

Additional caramel sauce, for topping (optional)

Instructions

1. Remove the caramel sauce packet from the box of flan and pour it into a lightly greased 9 x 9-inch (23 x 23 cm) square cake pan, spreading it out with a spoon or rubber spatula. You don't have to cover the entire pan; it will thin out and distribute evenly on its own.

2. Add milk and flan to a medium saucepan and whisk until combined. Sprinkle in gelatin and let it sit for a minute, letting the gelatin activate. Place saucepan over medium heat, whisking until gelatin dissolves. Bring to a light simmer, then remove from heat. Add the vodka or rum.

3. Pour mixture into the pan with the caramel sauce. Refrigerate for 2 hours, or until firm.

4. Carefully cut out shots with a shot glass or mini circle-shaped cookie or fondant cutter. Serve with the darker caramel side on top. Refrigerate until serving. If desired, top with additional caramel sauce before serving for a little extra sweetness and color.

TEQUILA SUNRISES

I absolutely love the ombré look of these shots. While a classic tequila sunrise recipe calls for grenadine, you could also use maraschino juice as a replacement. I often use maraschino cherries in my recipes, and this recipe makes sure that the juice doesn't go to waste.

 Makes 24 shots

Ingredients

6 oranges, halved horizontally

1 cup (240 mL) grenadine or maraschino cherry juice

4 x ¼-ounce (7 g) packet Knox gelatin, divided

¾ cup (180 mL) water

1¼ cups (300 mL) orange juice, divided

1 cup (240 mL) tequila

Instructions

1. To remove fruit from the orange rinds, carefully score around the insides of the rinds with a paring knife to loosen the citrus, then flip peels inside out and pull out the fruit. Line up rind halves on a baking sheet or place in a muffin tin so that they are secure and upright, and set aside.

2. Pour grenadine or maraschino cherry juice into a medium saucepan. Sprinkle in 2 packets gelatin and let it sit for 1 minute, letting the gelatin activate. Place saucepan over medium heat, whisking until gelatin dissolves. Bring to a light simmer, then remove from heat. Pour ¼ cup (60 mL) grenadine mixture into a separate cup or bowl and set aside.

3. Add water to remaining ¾ cup (180 mL) grenadine mixture. Pour this mixture into a spouted bowl or measuring cup, then carefully pour into orange halves, just covering the bottoms. Refrigerate for 30–60 minutes, or until sticky and slightly set but not firm.

4. Add ¼ cup (60 mL) orange juice to the ¼ cup (60 mL) grenadine mixture you set aside. Pour on top of the grenadine layer in your hollowed-out oranges, making a thin middle layer. This will give the shots an ombré or gradient effect. Refrigerate for 10–15 minutes.

5. Pour remaining 1 cup (240 mL) orange juice in a medium saucepan. Sprinkle in remaining 2 packets gelatin and let it sit for 1 minute, letting the gelatin activate. Place saucepan over medium heat, whisking until gelatin dissolves. Bring to a light simmer, then remove from heat. Add the tequila. Let mixture come to room temperature.

6. Pour this mixture on top of the two layers, filling the rest of the orange halves. Refrigerate for 2 hours, or until firm.

7. Slice halves in half. Refrigerate until serving.

STRAWBERRY MARGARITAS

These awesome shots take a little extra time to prepare but are totally worth it. The real strawberry flavor masks the tequila flavor. Plus, they are so much fun to pop right into your mouth.

 Makes 48 shots

Ingredients

2 pints (700 g) large strawberries

1 cup (240 mL) water

3-ounce (85 g) box strawberry Jell-O

1 cup (240 mL) tequila

Sugar, to taste

Lime, sliced, for garnish

Instructions

1. Slice the bottoms of the strawberries flat to allow them to stand upright. When you do so, make sure not to cut off so much that there is a hole—the slightest hole will allow the gelatin to leak out of the berries. Use a paring knife or small spoon to hollow out the strawberries as much as possible.

2. Place water in a medium saucepan, bring to a boil, and lower heat to medium. Add the Jell-O and whisk until powder dissolves. Remove from heat. Add the tequila.

3. Pour mixture into a spouted bowl or measuring cup, then carefully pour it into the strawberries. Refrigerate for 2 hours, or until firm.

4. Pour some sugar on a plate and rim your strawberries with it. You don't need to wet the berry; it will stick on its own. Refrigerate until serving. Garnish with the sliced lime before serving.

JALAPEÑO MARGARITAS

Some like it hot! If you do, then these tart and spicy margarita shots are for you. Dare your guests to try one! You can also cut out plain margarita shots with the leftover gelatin in the pan.

 Makes 18 shots

Ingredients

2 cups (480 mL) margarita mix, divided

4 x ¼-ounce (7 g) packet Knox gelatin, divided

2 cups (480 mL) tequila, divided

1 jalapeño, seeded and thinly sliced

½ cup (100 g) sugar

Instructions

1. Pour 1 cup (240 mL) margarita mix into a medium saucepan. Sprinkle in 2 packets Knox gelatin and let it sit for 1 minute, letting the gelatin activate. Place saucepan over medium heat, whisking until gelatin dissolves. Bring to a light simmer, then remove from heat. Add 1 cup (240 mL) tequila.

2. Pour mixture into a lightly greased 9 x 13-inch (23 x 33 cm) pan. Refrigerate for 30–60 minutes, or until sticky and slightly set but not firm. Combine sliced jalapeño with the sugar. Set aside.

3. Pour remaining 1 cup (240 mL) margarita mix into a medium saucepan. Sprinkle in remaining 2 packets gelatin and let it sit for 1 minute, letting the gelatin activate. Place saucepan over medium heat, whisking until gelatin dissolves. Bring to a light simmer, then remove from heat. Add remaining 1 cup (240 mL) tequila. Let mixture come to room temperature.

4. Pour mixture on top of first layer. Place sugared jalapeños in rows—with enough space to cut squares around them—in the mixture. Refrigerate for 2 hours, or until firm.

5. Carefully cut shots with a mini square-shaped cookie or fondant cutter or a knife and remove from pan. Refrigerate until serving.

Summer

KEY LIME PIES

LIME IN THE COCONUT

PINK LEMONADE

STRAWBERRY PATCH

STRAWBERRY SHORTCAKES

PEACH TARTS

PEACHES & CREAM

PIÑA COLADAS

RASPBERRY LEMONADE

RASPBERRY VODKA BITES

S'MORES

WATERMELONS

WATERMELONS ON A STICK

WATERMELON MOJITOS

SANGRIA

LEMON DROPS

4th of July

RED, WHITE & BLUE WITH CHERRIES

RED, WHITE & BLUEBERRY CAKES

RED, WHITE & BLUE BOMB POPS

KEY LIME PIES

These shots are creamy, sweet, and tart... just like key lime pie. Cruzan and Captain Morgan both make key lime–flavored rum and either brand will work perfectly.

 Makes 12–15 shots

Ingredients

1 cup (240 mL) water

3 tablespoons (45 mL) sweetened condensed milk

½ x 3.4 ounce (96 g) box Jell-O cheesecake instant pudding mix

2 x ¼-ounce (7 g) packet Knox gelatin

1 cup (240 mL) key lime–flavored rum

2 graham crackers, crushed

1 lime for zesting, for topping

Instructions

1. Add water and sweetened condensed milk to a medium saucepan and whisk until combined. Add cheesecake instant pudding mix and whisk again. Sprinkle in gelatin and let it sit for 1 minute, letting the gelatin activate.

2. Place saucepan over medium heat, whisking until gelatin dissolves. Bring to a light simmer, then remove from heat. Add the key lime–flavored rum.

3. Pour into a lightly greased 9 x 9-inch (23 x 23 cm) square cake pan. Refrigerate for 2 hours, or until firm.

4. Carefully cut out shots with a mini triangle-shaped cookie or fondant cutter and remove from pan. Gently dip one side of each shot into a small bowl of crushed graham crackers for the "crust." Refrigerate until serving. Top with lime zest before serving.

LIME IN THE COCONUT

"You put the lime in the coconut…" Yeah, I pretty much sang that the whole time I made these tropical delights.

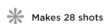 Makes 28 shots

Ingredients

7 limes, halved horizontally
½ cup (120 mL) Thai coconut milk
½ cup (120 mL) water
2 x ¼-ounce (7 g) packet Knox gelatin
¼ cup (50 g) sugar
1 cup (240 mL) whipped cream–flavored vodka
Toasted coconut, for serving (optional)
Lime wedges, for serving (optional)

Instructions

1. To remove fruit from the lime rinds, carefully score around the insides of the rinds with a paring knife to loosen the citrus, then flip peels inside out and pull out the fruit. Place rinds on a baking sheet or place in a muffin tin so they are secure and upright, and set aside.

2. Add coconut milk and water to a medium saucepan and whisk until combined. Sprinkle in gelatin and let it sit for 1 minute, letting the gelatin activate. Place saucepan over medium heat, whisking until gelatin dissolves.

3. Add the sugar and whisk until it dissolves. Bring to a light simmer, then remove from heat. Add the vodka.

4. Pour mixture into a spouted bowl or measuring cup, then carefully pour into lime halves. Save any leftover mixture in case you need to top off shots as they set. Refrigerate for 2 hours, or until set.

5. Slice lime halves in half. Refrigerate until serving. If desired, serve with toasted coconut and lime wedges.

PINK LEMONADE

Is there anything more summery than a glass of pink lemonade? How about boozy pink lemonade wedges?

 Makes 32 shots

Ingredients

8 lemons, halved horizontally

1 cup (240 mL) water

½ x 12-ounce (355 mL) can pink lemonade frozen concentrate

3 x ¼-ounce (7 g) packet Knox gelatin

Red or pink food coloring

1 cup (240 mL) vodka or alcohol of choice

Instructions

1. To remove fruit from the rinds, carefully score around the insides of the rinds with a paring knife to loosen the citrus, then flip peels inside out and pull out the fruit. Line up rind halves on a baking sheet or place in a muffin tin so that they are secure and upright, and set aside.

2. Add water and frozen concentrate to a medium saucepan and whisk until combined. Sprinkle in gelatin and let it sit for 1 minute, letting the gelatin activate. Place saucepan over medium heat, whisking until gelatin dissolves. Bring to a light simmer, then remove from heat.

3. Add red or pink food coloring for a brighter pink color. Add the vodka.

4. Pour mixture into a spouted bowl or measuring cup, then carefully pour it into the lemon halves. Save any leftover mixture in case you need to top off shots as they set. Refrigerate for 2 hours, or until firm.

5. Slice lemon halves in half. Refrigerate until serving.

STRAWBERRY PATCH

I came up with these shots when I was trying to find a fruit other than maraschino cherries to use in a recipe. These are easy to make and easy to pick up. Try making them with blue Jell-O for a 4th of July party.

 Makes 20 shots

Ingredients

2 cups (480 mL) water, divided

2 x 3-ounce (85 g) box strawberry Jell-O, divided

2 x ¼-ounce (7 g) packet Knox gelatin

2 cups (480 mL) strawberry- or whipped cream–flavored vodka, divided

20 medium or large strawberries with stems, halved horizontally

Instructions

1. Add 1 cup (240 mL) water and 1 box strawberry Jell-O to a medium saucepan and whisk until powder dissolves. Sprinkle in 1 packet gelatin and let it sit for 1 minute, letting the gelatin activate. Place saucepan over medium heat, whisking until gelatin dissolves. Bring to a light simmer, then remove from heat. Add 1 cup (240 mL) vodka.

2. Pour mixture into a lightly greased 9 x 13-inch (23 x 33 cm) pan. Refrigerate for 30–60 minutes, or until sticky and slightly set but not firm.

3. Repeat step 1. Let mixture come to room temperature.

4. Pour mixture on top of first layer. Place strawberry halves with stems in rows—with enough room to cut circles around them—in the mixture. Refrigerate for 2 hours, or until firm.

5. Carefully cut out shots around the strawberries with the rim of a shot glass or a mini circle-shaped cookie or fondant cutter and remove from pan. Refrigerate until serving.

STRAWBERRY SHORTCAKES

What's tastier than strawberry shortcake? How about a strawberry shortcake shot infused with cake-flavored vodka? This shot was my husband's idea, and it's delicious!

 Makes 24–48 shots

Ingredients

1 cup (240 mL) water

3-ounce (85 g) box strawberry Jell-O

1 cup (240 mL) cake-flavored vodka

2 packages premade shortcake "bowls" (12 cakes)

4 ounces (113 g) strawberry cream cheese

20 strawberries, trimmed (optional)

Instructions

1. Pour water into a medium saucepan, bring to a boil, and lower heat to medium. Add Jell-O and whisk until powder dissolves. Remove from heat. Add the vodka. Let mixture come to room temperature.

2. Coat the inside of each shortcake bowl with cream cheese—this acts as a barrier, preventing the mixture from being absorbed into the cakes.

3. Pour the mixture into the cake bowls on top of the cream cheese. Add a strawberry to the center of each bowl, if desired. Refrigerate for 2 hours, or until firm. Save any leftover mixture in case you need to top off cakes as they set, checking on cakes periodically.

4. Slice the rounded edges off each cake to make a square, then slice each cake into halves or quarters. Refrigerate until serving.

PEACH TARTS

Not only do these shots look gorgeous, but they also taste really good! They're sweet and sour with a sweet peach flavor combined with a bit of sour margarita mix. The swirled red food coloring really gives them a peachy effect.

 Makes 24 shots

Ingredients

2 cups (475 mL) margarita mix or lime juice

4 x ¼-ounce (7 g) packet Knox gelatin

Red and yellow food coloring

2 cups (475 mL) peach schnapps

24 fresh mint leaves, for topping

Instructions

1. Pour margarita mix or lime juice into a medium saucepan. Sprinkle in gelatin and let it sit for 1 minute, letting the gelatin activate. Place saucepan over medium heat, whisking until gelatin dissolves. Bring to a light simmer, then remove from heat.

2. Add 1 drop red food coloring and 1–2 drops yellow food coloring to get a light orange, peachy color. Add the peach schnapps.

3. Pour mixture into a lightly greased 9 x 13-inch (23 x 33 cm) pan. Add 1 drop red food coloring to the left and right sides of the pan. Using a toothpick, gently swirl around the coloring to give it the appearance of a peach. Do not overmix; you want to see defined swirls. Refrigerate for 2 hours, or until firm.

4. Run a mini heart-shaped cookie or fondant cutter under hot water for a minute or two to make it more pliable, then gently squeeze the sides so its shape resembles a peach.

5. Carefully cut out the shots with the peach-shaped cutter and remove from the pan. Refrigerate until serving. Top each shot with a small mint leaf before serving.

PEACHES & CREAM

Just when you thought there wasn't another way to hollow out fruit and fill it with booze, I came up with these delightful shots. When I first made these, I was afraid they would be too strong, but the fresh peach flavor overcomes the alcohol flavor. These are a triple threat: pretty, tasty, and strong. Be careful!

 Makes 16 shots

Ingredients

4 peaches, halved vertically and pits removed

3 tablespoons (45 mL) sweetened condensed milk

¼ cup (60 mL) water

2 x ¼-ounce (7 g) packet Knox gelatin

½ cup (120 mL) vodka

½ cup (120 mL) peach schnapps

Instructions

1. To remove fruit from the skins, use a melon baller or a spoon to hollow out most of the fruit, leaving only a thin layer of fruit around the skin. Line up skins on a baking sheet or place in a muffin tin so that they are secure and upright, and set aside. Also set aside the removed fruit.

2. Add removed fruit, sweetened condensed milk, and water to a food processor or blender. Puree the mixture until smooth. Push the pureed mixture through a fine mesh strainer to make sure it's extra smooth.

3. Pour 1 cup (240 mL) of the pureed mixture into a medium saucepan. Sprinkle in gelatin

and let it sit for 1 minute, letting the gelatin activate. Place saucepan over medium heat, whisking until gelatin dissolves. Bring to a light simmer, then remove from heat.

4. In a separate bowl, combine vodka and peach schnapps. Add the alcohol to the peach puree mixture.

5. Pour mixture into a spouted bowl or measuring cup, then carefully pour it into the peach halves. Refrigerate for 2 hours, or until firm.

6. Slice peach halves in half. Refrigerate until serving.

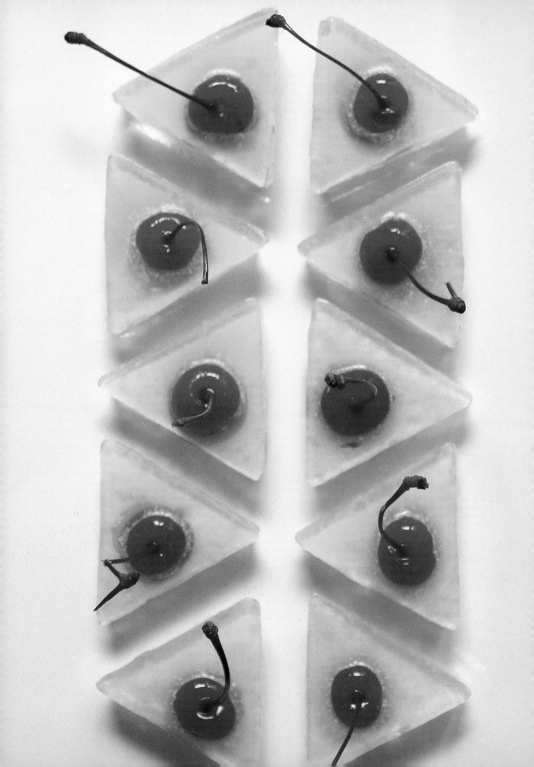

PIÑA COLADAS

"If you like piña coladas...," then these shots are for you. They're really easy to make and are the quintessential vacation flavor. Save any excess Jell-O and cut out fun shapes.

 Makes 20–24 shots

Ingredients

½ cup (120 mL) Thai coconut milk

1½ cups (360 mL) water, divided

3 x ¼-ounce (7 g) packet Knox gelatin, divided

¼ cup (50 g) sugar

1¾ cups (420 mL) Malibu Rum, divided

20–24 maraschino cherries with stems, halved horizontally

3-ounce (85 g) box island pineapple Jell-O

Instructions

1. To make the coconut layer, add Thai coconut milk and ½ cup (120 mL) water to a medium saucepan and whisk until combined. Sprinkle in 2 packets of gelatin and let it sit for 1 minute, letting the gelatin activate. Place saucepan over medium heat, whisking until gelatin dissolves.

2. Add the sugar and whisk until it dissolves. Bring to a light simmer, then remove from heat. Add 1 cup (240 mL) rum.

3. Pour the mixture into a lightly greased 9 x 13-inch (23 x 33 cm) pan. Refrigerate for 30–60 minutes, or until sticky and slightly set but not firm.

4. Place cherry halves with stems in rows—with enough space to cut triangles around them—on the set layer.

5. To make the pineapple layer, add 1 cup (240 mL) water and island pineapple Jell-O to a medium saucepan and whisk to combine. Sprinkle in 1 packet of gelatin and let it sit for 1 minute, letting the gelatin activate. Place saucepan over medium heat, whisking until gelatin dissolves. Bring to a light simmer, then remove from heat. Add ¾ cup (180 mL) rum. Let mixture come to room temperature.

6. Pour mixture over coconut layer. If any of the cherries move, carefully reposition them. Refrigerate for 2 hours, or until firm.

7. Carefully cut out the shots around the cherries with a mini triangle-shaped cookie or fondant cutter. Refrigerate until serving.

RASPBERRY LEMONADE

These are a simple and pretty take on a lemon-wedge shot. You can replace the raspberries with blueberries or strawberries—actually, any fruit will do.

 Makes 40 shots

Ingredients

10 lemons, halved horizontally

1 cup (240 mL) lemonade

2 x ¼-ounce (7 g) packet Knox gelatin

1 cup (240 mL) citrus-flavored vodka

1 pint (310 g) raspberries

Instructions

1. To remove fruit from the lemon rinds, carefully score around the insides of the rinds with a paring knife to loosen the citrus, then flip peels inside out and pull out the fruit. Line up rind halves on a baking sheet or place in a muffin tin so that they are secure and upright, and set aside.

2. Pour lemonade into a medium saucepan. Sprinkle in gelatin, and let it sit for 1 minute, letting the gelatin activate. Place saucepan over medium heat, whisking until gelatin dissolves. Bring to a light simmer, then remove from heat. Add the vodka.

3. Pour mixture into a spouted bowl or measuring cup, then carefully pour it into the lemon halves. Drop in the raspberries. Refrigerate for 2 hours, or until firm.

4. Slice lemon halves in half. Refrigerate until serving.

RASPBERRY VODKA BITES

Be careful with these little bites: they are addictive and you hardly notice the vodka! Serve them in a bowl or place them in a cocktail for an extra-boozy surprise.

 Makes 100 shots

Ingredients

½ cup (120 mL) lemon juice

½ cup (120 mL) water

2 x ¼-ounce (7 g) packet Knox gelatin

½ cup (100 g) sugar

1 cup (240 mL) vodka flavor of choice

2 pints (620 g) or 100 raspberries

Instructions

1. Add lemon juice and water to a medium saucepan and whisk until combined. Sprinkle in gelatin and let it sit for 1 minute, letting the gelatin activate. Place saucepan over medium heat, whisking until gelatin dissolves. Add the sugar and whisk until it dissolves. Bring to a light simmer, then remove from heat. Add the vodka.

2. Align raspberries upright in a muffin tin, fitting as many raspberries as you can into each cup, side by side. Carefully spoon in the mixture into the cavities of the raspberries. Refrigerate for 2 hours, or until firm.

3. Refrigerate until serving.

S'MORES

I couldn't make marshmallow shots (see page 31) without trying a s'more shot, too. These fun shots have chocolate vodka inside large marshmallows, with graham cracker crumbs dusting the sides. They're a little bit more work to make, but if you're up for the challenge, it's totally worth it.

 Makes 24–30 shots

Ingredients

28-ounce (793 g) bag large marshmallows

1 cup (240 mL) water

1 tablespoon (28 g) hot chocolate mix

2 x ¼-ounce (7 g) packet Knox gelatin

1 cup (240 mL) chocolate-flavored vodka

1 cup (130 g) baking chocolate or 1 cup (175 g) chocolate chips, melted

1 cup (84 g) crushed graham crackers

Instructions

1. Use a melon baller to hollow out or clean fingers to pinch out the centers of the marshmallows. Let marshmallows sit out for 1–2 hours to harden.

2. Add water and hot chocolate mix to a medium saucepan and whisk until combined. Sprinkle in gelatin and let it sit for 1 minute, letting the gelatin activate. Place saucepan over medium heat, whisking until gelatin dissolves. Bring to a light simmer, then remove from heat. Add the vodka.

3. This step is really important. Let the mixture cool. It should be at least room temperature before you pour it into the marshmallows—if it's hot, it will melt the marshmallow and it won't work.

4. Pour mixture into a spouted bowl or measuring cup, then carefully pour it into the hardened, hollowed-out marshmallows. Save any leftover mixture in case you need to top off shots as they set. Refrigerate for 2 hours, or until firm.

5. Refrigerate until serving. To serve, dip the marshmallows into the melted chocolate, then roll the marshmallows in crushed graham crackers.

WATERMELONS

This was the first shot recipe I ever made. These mini watermelons were featured in *Bon Appétit*, which really inspired me to keep trying unique shot creations and to push the limits. These are perfect for summer barbecues or any summer gathering.

 Makes 40 shots

Ingredients

10 limes, halved horizontally

1 cup (240 mL) water

3-ounce (85 g) box watermelon Jell-O or red Jell-O flavor of your choice

¼-ounce (7 g) packet Knox gelatin

1 cup (240 mL) vodka or alcohol of choice

Instructions

1. To remove fruit from the lime rinds, carefully score around the insides of the rinds with a paring knife to loosen the citrus, then flip peels inside out and pull out the fruit. Line up rind halves on a baking sheet or place in a muffin tin so that they are secure and upright, and set aside.

2. Add water and watermelon Jell-O to a medium saucepan and whisk until powder dissolves. Sprinkle in gelatin and let it sit for 1 minute, letting the gelatin activate. Place saucepan over medium heat, whisking until gelatin dissolves. Bring to a light simmer, then remove from heat. Add the vodka.

3. Pour mixture into a spouted bowl or measuring cup, then carefully pour it into the lime halves. Save any leftover mixture in case you need to top off shots as they set. Refrigerate for 2 hours, or until firm.

4. Slice the lime halves in half. Refrigerate until serving.

WATERMELONS ON A STICK

I was inspired to make these shots when I saw real watermelon served on a popsicle stick one day. These call for red Jell-O, but they would also look pretty with pink Jell-O. Save the leftover gelatin from each layer and make individual shots if you don't want to waste it.

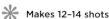 Makes 12–14 shots

Ingredients

2½ cups (600 mL) water, divided

3-ounce (85 g) box green Jell-O

2½ x ¼-ounce (7 g) packet Knox gelatin, divided

2 cups (480 mL) tequila, divided

1 tablespoon (15 mL) sweetened condensed milk

3-ounce (85 g) box red or pink Jell-O

12–14 popsicle sticks

Instructions

1. To make the green layer, add 1 cup (240 mL) water and green Jell-O to a medium saucepan and whisk until combined. Sprinkle in 1 packet of gelatin and let it sit for 1 minute, letting the gelatin activate. Place saucepan over medium heat, whisking until gelatin dissolves. Bring to a light simmer, then remove from heat. Add 1 cup (240 mL) tequila.

2. Pour half of the mixture into a lightly greased 7½ x 3½-inch (19 x 9 cm) loaf pan. (You can discard the rest of the mixture or use to make plain shots.) Refrigerate for 30–60 minutes, or until sticky and slightly set but not firm.

3. To make the white layer, add ¼ cup (60 mL) water and the condensed milk to a small saucepan and whisk until combined. Sprinkle in ½ packet of gelatin and let it sit for 1 minute, letting the gelatin activate. Place saucepan over medium heat, whisking until gelatin dissolves. Bring to a light simmer, then remove from heat. Add ¼ cup (60 mL) water. Let mixture come to room temperature.

4. Pour this mixture on top of the green layer. This layer should be very thin. Refrigerate for 10–15 minutes.

5. To make the red or pink layer, repeat step 1 with the red or pink Jell-O. Let mixture come to room temperature.

6. Pour half of the red mixture on top of the thin white layer. (You can discard the rest of the mixture or use to make plain shots.) Refrigerate for 2 hours, or until firm.

7. Using a rubber spatula or butter knife, run it along the edge of the loaf pan to loosen the gelatin. Flip the pan onto a cutting board, releasing the gelatin whole. Carefully cut out shots with a mini triangle-shaped cookie or fondant cutter, with the green layer as the triangle base.

8. Securely place popsicle sticks into green layer. Refrigerate until serving.

WATERMELON MOJITOS

I had the best mojito of my life while I was in the Outer Banks one summer, which inspired this recipe. These shots have two layers: a layer of real watermelon juice with sugar and a layer of white rum with freshly chopped mint leaves.

 Makes 24 shots

Ingredients

½ small seedless watermelon

4 x ¼-ounce (7 g) packet Knox gelatin, divided

½ cup (100 g) sugar (or to desired sweetness), divided

2 cups (480 mL) water, divided

1 cup (240 mL) white rum

Handful fresh mint, chopped

Instructions

1. In a blender or food processor, puree enough watermelon to equal 1 cup (240 mL) juice. Push the watermelon puree through a fine mesh to make it extra smooth.

2. Pour the watermelon juice into a medium saucepan. Sprinkle in 2 packets gelatin and let it sit for 1 minute, letting the gelatin activate. Place saucepan over medium heat, whisking until gelatin dissolves. Add ¼ cup (50 g) sugar and whisk until it dissolves. Bring to a light simmer, then remove from heat. Add 1 cup (240 mL) water.

3. Pour mixture into a lightly greased 9 x 13-inch (23 x 33 cm) pan. Refrigerate for 30–60 minutes, or until sticky and slightly set but not firm.

4. Pour 1 cup (240 mL) water into a medium saucepan. Sprinkle in 2 packets gelatin and let it sit for 1 minute, letting the gelatin activate. Place saucepan over medium heat, whisking until gelatin dissolves.

5. Add ¼ cup (50 g) sugar and whisk until it dissolves. Bring to a light simmer, then remove from heat. Add the white rum and chopped mint. Let mixture come to room temperature.

6. Pour mixture into pan on top of the watermelon layer. Refrigerate for 2 hours, or until firm.

7. Carefully cut out shots with the rim of a shot glass or a mini circle-shaped cookie or fondant cutter and remove from pan. Press down slowly, making sure you don't have any mint leaves caught on it when you move on to the next. Refrigerate until serving.

SANGRIA

Sangria is my all-time favorite summer drink. I like to make it in the winter, too. These shots play on all of the colors and flavors of classic sangria by using lemon, orange, and lime rinds and real fruit inside. For a white sangria, swap out the red wine with a Moscato or sauvignon blanc, and the apples and strawberries with peaches and raspberries.

 Makes 24 shots

Ingredients

2 oranges, halved horizontally

2 lemons, halved horizontally

2 limes, halved horizontally

1 cup (240 mL) red wine of choice

2 x ¼-ounce (7 g) packet Knox gelatin

¾ cup (180 mL) apple juice

¼ cup (60 mL) raspberry- or blueberry-flavored vodka

10 strawberries, sliced

½ green apple, diced

Instructions

1. To remove fruit from the fruit rinds, carefully score around the insides of the rinds with a paring knife to loosen the citrus, then flip peels inside out and pull out the fruit. Line up rind halves on a baking sheet or place in a muffin tin so that they are secure and upright, and set aside.

2. Pour red wine into a medium saucepan. Sprinkle in gelatin and let it sit for 1 minute, letting it activate. Place saucepan over medium heat, whisking until gelatin dissolves. Bring to a light simmer, then remove from heat. Add the apple juice and vodka.

3. Pour mixture into a spouted bowl or measuring cup, then carefully pour it into the fruit halves. Carefully drop in strawberries and apples. Refrigerate for 2 hours, or until firm.

4. Slice fruit halves in half. Refrigerate until serving.

LEMON DROPS

These shots are an easy adaptation of a yummy, classic shot. I like to serve these with a bowl of sugar in the middle of the serving tray so you can dip the wedge in before popping it into your mouth.

 Makes 32 shots

Ingredients

8 lemons, halved horizontally

1 cup (240 mL) freshly squeezed lemon juice (about 5–6 lemons)

2 x ¼-ounce (7 g) packet Knox gelatin

2 cups (400 g) sugar, divided

1 cup (240 mL) citrus-flavored vodka

Instructions

1. To remove fruit from the lemon rinds, carefully score around the insides of the rinds with a paring knife to loosen the citrus, then flip peels inside out and pull out the fruit. Line up rind halves on a baking sheet or place in a muffin tin so that they are secure and upright, and set aside. Save the lemon juice from the fruit in a separate bowl.

2. Pour lemon juice into a medium saucepan. Sprinkle in gelatin and let it sit for 1 minute, letting the gelatin activate. Place saucepan over medium heat, whisking until gelatin dissolves. Add 1 cup (200 g) sugar and whisk until it dissolves. Bring to a light simmer, then remove from heat. Add the vodka.

3. Pour mixture into spouted bowl or measuring cup, then carefully pour the mixture into the lemon halves. Refrigerate for 2 hours, or until firm.

4. Slice lemon halves in half. Refrigerate until serving. Serve with a small dish of remaining 1 cup (200 g) sugar on the side, for dipping.

RED, WHITE & BLUE WITH CHERRIES

These patriotic shots are the perfect thing for 4th of July parties. Pick up the shot by the cherry stem and enjoy.

 Makes 15–24 shots

Ingredients

2½ cups (600 mL) water, divided

3-ounce (85 g) box cherry Jell-O

4 x ¼-ounce (7 g) packet Knox gelatin, divided

3 cups (720 mL) cherry-, whipped cream–, or cake-flavored vodka, divided

½ cup (120 mL) Thai coconut milk

3 tablespoons (38 g) sugar

15–24 maraschino cherries with stems, halved horizontally

3-ounce (85 g) box blue Jell-O

Instructions

1. To make the red layer, add 1 cup (240 mL) water and cherry Jell-O to a medium saucepan and whisk to combine. Sprinkle in 1 packet gelatin and let it sit for 1 minute, letting the gelatin activate. Place saucepan over medium heat, whisking until gelatin dissolves. Bring to a light simmer, then remove from heat. Add 1 cup (240 mL) vodka.

2. Pour mixture into a lightly greased 9 x 13-inch (23 x 33 cm) pan. Refrigerate for 30–60 minutes, or until sticky and slightly set but not firm.

3. To make the white layer, add ½ cup (120 mL) water and Thai coconut milk to a medium saucepan and whisk to combine. Sprinkle in 2 packets gelatin and let it sit for 1 minute, letting the gelatin activate. Place saucepan over medium heat, whisking until gelatin dissolves. Add the sugar and whisk until it dissolves. Bring to a light simmer, then remove from heat. Add 1 cup (240 mL) vodka. Let mixture come to room temperature.

4. Pour on top of red layer. Place cherry halves with stems in rows—with enough space to cut squares around them—in the white mixture. Refrigerate for 30–60 minutes, or until sticky and slightly set but not firm.

5. To make the blue layer, repeat step 1 with the blue Jell-O. Let mixture come to room temperature.

6. Pour on top of white layer. Refrigerate for 2 hours, or until firm.

7. Carefully cut out shots around the cherries with a mini square-shaped cookie or fondant cutter or a knife and remove from pan. Refrigerate until serving.

RED, WHITE & BLUEBERRY CAKES

I love the flavors of this shot. The blueberry schnapps and cake-flavored vodka are a unique combination. If you want something red, white, and blue that isn't so literal, this shot is perfect.

 Makes 20–24 shots

Ingredients

1 cup (145 g) blueberries

2 cups (480 mL) water, divided

4 tablespoons (50 g) sugar

4 x ¼-ounce (7 g) packet Knox gelatin, divided

1 cup (240 mL) blueberry schnapps or crème de cassis

3 tablespoons (45 mL) sweetened condensed milk

1 cup (240 mL) cake-flavored vodka

20–24 maraschino cherries, halved horizontally

Instructions

1. To make the blue layer, puree blueberries, 1 cup (240 mL) water, and sugar in a food processor or blender. Push mixture through a fine mesh strainer to make extra smooth and remove any pulp. Pour mixture into a medium saucepan. Sprinkle in 2 packets gelatin and let it sit for 1 minute, letting the gelatin activate. Place saucepan over medium heat, whisking until gelatin dissolves. Bring to a light simmer, then remove from heat. Add the blueberry schnapps or crème de cassis.

2. Pour into a lightly greased 9 x 13-inch (23 x 33 cm) pan. Refrigerate for 30–60 minutes, or until sticky and slightly set but not firm.

3. To make the white layer, add 1 cup (240 mL) water and sweetened condensed milk to a medium saucepan. Sprinkle in 2 packets gelatin and let sit for 1 minute, letting the gelatin activate. Place saucepan over medium heat, whisking until gelatin dissolves. Bring to a light simmer, then remove from heat. Add the cake-flavored vodka. Let mixture come to room temperature.

4. Pour mixture on top of blue layer in pan. Place cherry halves with stems in rows—with enough space to cut triangles around them—in the white mixture. Refrigerate for 2 hours, or until firm.

5. Carefully cut out shots around the cherries with a mini triangle-shaped cookie or fondant cutter and remove from pan. Refrigerate until serving.

RED, WHITE & BLUE BOMB POPS

These delicious shots are an adult spin on an ice-cream truck classic. Adorable and patriotic, they are fun to eat, and the combination of cotton candy–flavored vodka and blue raspberry Jell-O is delectable.

 Makes 12–15 shots

Ingredients

1⅓ cups (320 mL) water, divided

3-ounce (85 g) box blue raspberry Jell-O

1⅓ cups (320 mL) + ½ cup (120 mL) cotton candy–flavored vodka, divided

½ cup (120 mL) Thai coconut milk

¼-ounce (7 g) packet Knox gelatin

2 tablespoons (25 g) sugar

3-ounce (85 g) box cherry Jell-O

12–15 popsicle sticks

Instructions

1. To make the blue layer, pour ⅔ cup (160 mL) water into a medium saucepan, bring to a boil, and lower heat to medium. Add blue raspberry Jell-O and whisk until powder dissolves. Remove from heat. Add ⅔ cup (160 mL) vodka.

2. Pour mixture into a lightly greased 7½ x 3½-inch (19 x 9 cm) loaf pan. Refrigerate for 30–60 minutes, or until sticky and slightly set but not firm.

3. To make the white layer, pour Thai coconut milk into a medium saucepan. Sprinkle in gelatin and let it sit for 1 minute, letting the gelatin activate. Place saucepan over medium heat, whisking until gelatin dissolves. Add the sugar and whisk until it dissolves. Bring to a light simmer, then remove from heat. Add ½ cup (120 mL) vodka. Let mixture come to room temperature.

4. Pour mixture on top of blue layer in pan. Refrigerate for 30–60 minutes, or until sticky and slightly set but not firm.

5. To make the red layer, repeat step 1 with the cherry Jell-O. Let mixture come to room temperature.

6. Pour mixture on top of white layer in pan. Refrigerate for 2 hours, or until firm.

7. Using a rubber spatula or butter knife, run it along the edge of the loaf pan to loosen the gelatin. Flip the pan onto a cutting board, releasing the gelatin whole. Slice gelatin as if you were slicing bread. Carefully cut out shots with a mini triangle-shaped cookie or fondant cutter, with the blue layer as the triangle base.

8. Securely place popsicle sticks into bottom blue layer. Refrigerate until serving.

Halloween

CARAMEL APPLES
CARAMEL APPLE SQUARES
CANDY APPLES
CANDY CORN

Thanksgiving

SPICED RUM & ROOT BEER
PUMPKIN PIES
PUMPKIN SPICE LATTES
CHERRY PIES
SUGARED CRANBERRY

CARAMEL APPLES

This is, hands down, my most famous shot. When I first made these, I had no idea how many people across the world would be making them for fall celebrations. The flavor combination of the crisp, tart apple and the sweet, gooey, rich caramel gets me every time.

 Makes 40 shots

Ingredients

10 small Granny Smith apples, halved vertically

1 lemon, halved horizonally, for juicing

½ cup (120 mL) water

1 tablespoon (28 g) caramel or regular hot chocolate mix

½ cup (120 mL) Thai coconut milk or regular milk

2 x ¼-ounce (7 g) packet Knox gelatin

¼ cup (50 g) sugar

Yellow food coloring

1 cup (240 mL) butterscotch schnapps or caramel-flavored vodka

Instructions

1. Using a melon baller, hollow out the centers of the apples. Squeeze lemon juice onto apple interiors to reduce browning. Line up apple halves on a baking sheet or place in a muffin tin so they are secure and upright, and set aside.

2. Add the water and hot chocolate mix to a medium saucepan and whisk to combine. Add milk and whisk again. Sprinkle in gelatin and let it sit for 1 minute, letting the gelatin activate. Place saucepan over medium heat, whisking until gelatin dissolves.

3. Add the sugar and whisk until it dissolves. Bring to a light simmer, then remove from heat. Add the yellow food coloring until you get desired caramel color (I use 3–4 drops). Add the schnapps or vodka.

4. Pour mixture into spouted bowl or measuring cup, then carefully pour it into apple halves. Refrigerate for 2 hours, or until firm.

5. Slice apple halves in half. Serve immediately—the lemon juice can only prevent browning for so long. Trim off parts of the apples that have browned too much.

CARAMEL APPLE SQUARES

In the past, I have been iffy about caramel apple treats that use artificial green apple flavor instead of real apple flavor. But then I tried some green apple licorice with caramel inside and there was no turning back!

 Makes 24–30 shots

Ingredients

1½ cups (360 mL) water, divided

1 tablespoons (28 g) caramel hot chocolate mix

½ cup (120 mL) evaporated milk

3 x ¼-ounce (7 g) packet Knox gelatin, divided

¼ cup (50 g) sugar

Yellow food coloring

2 cups (480 mL) caramel-flavored vodka or butterscotch schnapps, divided

2.79-ounce (79 g) box Jolly Rancher Green Apple Gelatin mix

Instructions

1. To make caramel layer, add ½ cup (120 mL) water and hot chocolate mix to a medium saucepan and whisk to combine. Add the evaporated milk and whisk again. Sprinkle in 2 packets gelatin and let it sit for 1 minute, letting the gelatin activate. Place saucepan over medium heat, whisking until gelatin dissolves.

2. Add sugar and whisk until it dissolves. Add the yellow food coloring until you get the desired caramel color (I use 2–3 drops). Bring to a light simmer, then remove from heat. Add 1 cup (240 mL) vodka or schnapps.

3. Pour mixture into a lightly greased 9 x 13-inch (23 x 33 cm) pan. Refrigerate for 30–60 minutes, or until sticky and slightly set but not firm.

4. To make green apple layer, add 1 cup (240 mL) water and green apple gelatin mix to a medium saucepan. Sprinkle in 1 packet gelatin and let it sit for 1 minute, letting the gelatin activate. Place saucepan over medium heat, whisking until gelatin dissolves. Bring to a light simmer, then remove from heat. Add 1 cup (240 mL) vodka or schnapps. Let mixture come to room temperature.

5. Pour mixture on top of caramel layer. Refrigerate for 2 hours, or until firm.

6. Carefully cut out shots with a mini square-shaped cookie or fondant cutter or a knife and remove from pan. Refrigerate until serving.

CANDY APPLES

If you love sticky, shiny, sweet candy apples instead of caramel apples, this shot is for you! The combination of cherry Jell-O with cinnamon schnapps really does taste just like them.

 Makes 40 shots

Ingredients

10 small red apples, halved vertically

1 lemon, halved horizontally, for juicing

1 cup (240 mL) water

3-ounce (85 g) box cherry Jell-O

¼-ounce (7 g) packet Knox gelatin

1 cup (240 mL) Goldschläger or cinnamon schnapps

Instructions

1. Using a melon baller, hollow out the centers of apples. Squeeze lemon juice onto apple interiors to reduce browning. Line up apple halves on a baking sheet or place in a muffin tin so they are secure and upright, and set aside.

2. Add the water and Jell-O to a medium saucepan and whisk to combine. Sprinkle in gelatin and let it sit for 1 minute, letting the gelatin activate. Place saucepan over medium heat, whisking until gelatin dissolves. Bring to a light simmer, then remove from heat. Add Goldschläger or schnapps.

3. Pour mixture into spouted bowl or measuring cup, then carefully pour it into apple halves. Refrigerate for 2 hours, or until firm.

4. Slice apple halves in half. Serve immediately—the lemon juice can only prevent the browning for so long. Trim off parts of the apples that have browned too much.

CANDY CORN

What's orange and white, jiggly, and tastes like a Creamsicle? Candy corn shots! These are the perfect thing for Halloween or fall parties.

 Makes 40 shots

Ingredients

10 oranges, halved horizontally

1½ cups (360 mL) water, divided

3-ounce (85 g) box orange Jell-O

2 cups (480 mL) whipped cream–flavored vodka, divided

½ cup (120 mL) Thai coconut milk

2 x ¼–ounce (7 g) packet Knox gelatin

¼ cup (100 g) sugar

Instructions

1. To remove fruit from the rinds, carefully score around the insides of the rinds with a paring knife to loosen the citrus, then flip peels inside out and pull out the fruit. Line up rind halves on a baking sheet or place in a muffin tin so they are secure and upright, and set aside.

2. To make the orange layer, pour 1 cup (240 mL) water into a medium saucepan, bring to a boil, and lower heat to medium. Add the orange Jell-O and whisk until powder dissolves. Remove from heat. Add 1 cup (240 mL) vodka.

3. Pour mixture into spouted bowl or measuring cup, then carefully pour it into orange halves, filling them halfway. Refrigerate for 30–60 minutes, or until sticky and slightly set but not firm.

4. To make the white layer, add ½ cup (120 mL) water and coconut milk to a medium saucepan and whisk until combined. Sprinkle in gelatin and let it sit for 1 minute, letting the gelatin activate. Place saucepan over medium heat, whisking until gelatin dissolves. Add the sugar and whisk until it dissolves. Bring to a light simmer, then remove from heat. Add 1 cup (240 mL) vodka. Let mixture come to room temperature.

5. Pour mixture into a spouted bowl or measuring cup, then carefully pour it on top of the orange layer. Refrigerate for 2 hours, or until firm.

6. Slice orange halves in half. Refrigerate until serving.

SPICED RUM & ROOT BEER

Are you ready for some football? I know my husband is. These shots are super easy and so much fun for football-viewing parties.

 Makes 12–15 shots

Ingredients

2 cups (475 mL) root beer

4 x ¼-ounce (7 g) packet Knox gelatin

2 cups (475 mL) Captain Morgan Spiced Rum

Small tube white icing

Instructions

1. Pour root beer into a medium saucepan. Sprinkle in gelatin and let it sit for 1 minute, letting the gelatin activate. Place saucepan over medium heat, whisking until gelatin dissolves. Bring to a light simmer, then remove from heat. Add the rum.

2. Pour mixture into a lightly greased 9 x 13-inch (23 x 33 cm) pan and refrigerate for 2 hours, or until firm.

3. Run a mini round-shaped cookie or fondant cutter under hot water for a minute or two to make it more pliable, then gently squeeze the top of the cutter (not at the seam) to form a football shape. You can also use a knife to cut free-form football shapes.

4. Carefully cut out shots and remove from pan. Use the white icing to pipe laces onto each football. Refrigerate until serving.

PUMPKIN PIES

I have a friend who makes these shots for her holiday party every year, and they taste just like pumpkin pie. You can find the mini graham-cracker piecrusts in the baking aisle of your grocery store.

 Makes 24 shots

Ingredients

1¼ cups (300 mL) water, divided

¼-ounce (7 g) packet Knox gelatin

⅓ cup (90 g) canned pumpkin pie mix

¼ cup (50 g) sugar

½ cup (120 mL) rum

½ tablespoon (7.5 mL) heavy cream

6 mini graham-cracker piecrusts

Whipped cream, for topping

Instructions

1. Pour 1 cup (240 mL) water into a medium saucepan. Sprinkle in gelatin and let it sit for 1 minute, letting the gelatin activate. Place saucepan over medium heat, whisking until gelatin dissolves.

2. Add pumpkin pie mix and sugar and whisk until sugar dissolves. Bring to a light simmer, then remove from heat.

3. In a separate bowl, combine rum, remaining ¼ cup (60 mL) water, and heavy cream. Add to pumpkin mixture.

4. Pour mixture into piecrusts. Refrigerate for 2 hours, or until firm.

5. Slice pies into quarters. Refrigerate until serving. Top with whipped cream before serving.

PUMPKIN SPICE LATTES

As soon as the weather starts to cool down, people start going crazy for pumpkin spice lattes. So these shots are sure to be a hit at any fall party. If you can't find vanilla- or caramel-flavored coffee, you can always use regular coffee.

 Makes 12 large shots

Ingredients

1 cup (240 mL) vanilla- or caramel-flavored coffee, cold

2 x ¼-ounce (7 g) packet Knox gelatin

3 tablespoons (45 mL) sweetened condensed milk

1 teaspoon (5 mL) to 1 tablespoon (15 mL) pumpkin pie spice, plus additional for topping

1 cup (240 mL) whipped cream–flavored vodka

12 straws (optional)

Whipped cream, for topping

Instructions

1. Pour coffee into a medium saucepan. Sprinkle in gelatin and let it sit for 1 minute, letting the gelatin activate. Place saucepan over medium heat, whisking until gelatin dissolves.

2. Add sweetened condensed milk and whisk until combined. Add pumpkin pie spice— amount will depend on how much spice you like—and whisk again. Bring to a light simmer, then remove from heat. Add the vodka.

3. Pour mixture into shot glasses and add straws, if you like. Refrigerate for 2 hours, or until firm.

4. Refrigerate until serving. Top with whipped cream and a sprinkle of pumpkin pie spice before serving.

CHERRY PIES

Though I specifically made these shots as cherry pie, you could always substitute any flavor of Jell-O for whatever kind of pie you want. These are perfect for holiday parties and would be cute for summer parties, too.

 Makes 24 shots

Ingredients

1 cup (240 mL) water

3-ounce (85 g) box cherry or black cherry Jell-O

1 cup (240 mL) cherry- or whipped cream–flavored vodka

6 mini graham-cracker piecrusts

Whipped cream, for topping

Instructions

1. Pour water into a medium saucepan, bring to a boil, and lower heat to medium. Add Jell-O and whisk until powder dissolves. Remove from heat and let cool slightly. Add the vodka.

2. Pour mixture into piecrusts. Refrigerate for 2 hours, or until firm.

3. Slice pies into quarters. Refrigerate until serving. Top with whipped cream before serving.

SUGARED CRANBERRY

Cranberries and Thanksgiving go hand in hand. And cranberry and vodka is a classic cocktail. Impress your holiday guest with this easy, pretty, and boozy adaptation.

 Makes 24–30 shots

Ingredients

2 cups (475 mL) cranberry juice

2 cups (400 g) sugar

4 x ¼-ounce (7 g) packet Knox gelatin

2 cups (475 mL) cranberry-flavored vodka

12–15 sugared cranberries, halved horizontally (optional), for topping

Zest from 1 orange, for topping

Instructions

1. Add cranberry juice and sugar to a medium saucepan and whisk to combine. Sprinkle in gelatin and let it sit for 1 minute, letting the gelatin activate. Place saucepan over medium heat, whisking until sugar and gelatin are dissolved. Bring to a light simmer, then remove from heat. Add the vodka.

2. Pour mixture into a lightly greased 9 x 13-inch (23 x 33 cm) pan. Refrigerate for 2 hours, or until firm.

3. Carefully cut out shots with a mini square-shaped cookie or fondant cutter or a knife and remove from pan. Refrigerate until serving. Top each one with a sugared cranberry, if desired, and orange zest before serving.

Christmas

GINGERBREAD MEN

APPLE CIDER & BUTTERED RUM

EGGNOG

EGGNOG PUDDINGS

CHRISTMAS TREES

CANDY CANES

TROPICAL WINTER

PEPPERMINT MOCHAS

SUGAR COOKIES

New Year's Eve

CHAMPAGNE & STRAWBERRIES

GRAPEFRUIT & PROSECCO

PEACH & VANILLA CHAMPAGNE

GINGERBREAD MEN

This gingerbread shot recipe is easy and delicious! If you can't find the Duncan Hines frosting packet—it's seasonal—gingerbread spice mix will do the trick.

 Makes 15–20 shots

Ingredients

2 cups (480 mL) water, divided

6 tablespoons (90 mL) sweetened condensed milk, divided

$\frac{1}{10}$-ounce (3 g) packet Duncan Hines Frosting Creations mix, gingerbread flavor, or 3 tablespoons (21 g) gingerbread spice mix, divided

4 x $\frac{1}{4}$-ounce (7 g) packet Knox gelatin, divided

2 cups (475 mL) vanilla-, whipped cream–, or cake-flavored vodka, divided

15–20 maraschino cherries with stems, halved horizontally

30–40 white nonpareil ball sprinkles (optional)

Instructions

1. Add 1 cup (240 mL) water and 3 tablespoons (45 mL) sweetened condensed milk to a medium saucepan, whisk to combine, and bring to a boil. Lower the heat and add half packet of Frosting Creations mix or 1½ tablespoons (10.5 g) gingerbread spice and combine. (Taste with a spoon to make sure it's sweet enough; if it's not, add a few tablespoons of sugar and boil again until combined.)

2. Remove from heat and let mixture cool completely. Sprinkle in 2 packets gelatin and let it sit for 1 minute, letting the gelatin activate. Place saucepan over medium heat, whisking until gelatin dissolves. Bring to a light simmer, then remove from heat. Add the vodka.

3. Pour mixture into a lightly greased 9 x 13-inch (23 x 33 cm) pan. Refrigerate for 30–60 minutes, or until sticky and slightly set but not firm.

4. Place cherry halves with stems in rows—with enough space to cut gingerbread-men shapes around them—on set layer.

5. Repeat steps 1–2. Pour this mixture on top of the first layer. Reposition any cherries that move. Refrigerate for 2 hours, or until firm.

6. Cut out shots around cherries with a mini gingerbread-shaped cookie or fondant cutter—wiggle the cutter around to make sure the edges are separated—and remove from pan. Place eyes on gingerbread men with the nonpareil sprinkles, if desired. Refrigerate until serving.

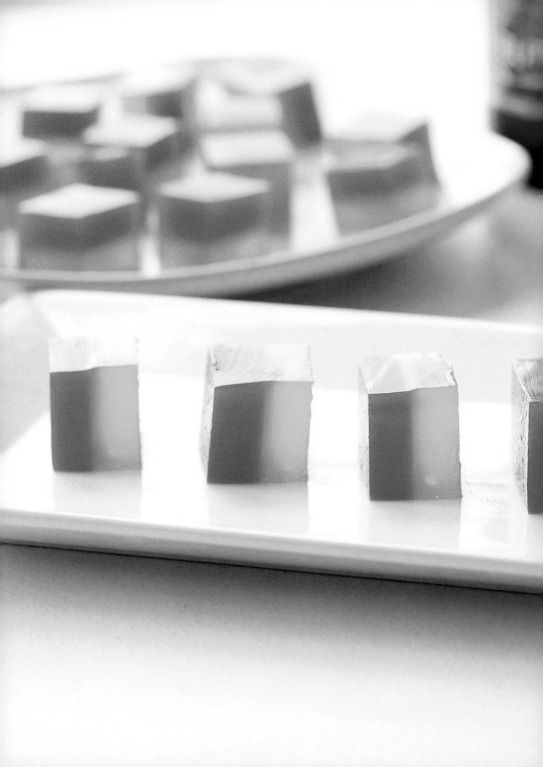

APPLE CIDER & BUTTERED RUM

Mmm, buttered rum. To achieve a lovely color difference in the layers of this shot, I add red food coloring to the apple cider—apple cider and buttered rum are actually very similar in color.

 Makes 25 shots

Ingredients

3 cups (720 mL) apple cider

Red food coloring

4 x ¼-ounce (7 g) packet Knox gelatin, divided

¾ cup (180 mL) butterscotch schnapps

¼ cup (60 mL) light rum

Instructions

1. Pour 1 cup (240 mL) apple cider into a medium saucepan. Add red food coloring until you get desired red color (I use 3–5 drops). Sprinkle in 2 packets gelatin and let it sit for 1 minute, letting the gelatin activate. Place saucepan over medium heat, whisking until gelatin dissolves. Bring to a light simmer, then remove from heat.

2. Pour 1 cup (240 mL) apple cider into a small bowl. Add 3–5 drops of red food coloring. Add cold cider to hot-cider mixture. Pour into a lightly greased 9 x 9-inch (23 x 23 cm) square cake pan. Refrigerate 30–60 minutes, or until sticky and slightly set but not firm.

3. Pour 1 cup (240 mL) apple cider into a medium saucepan. Sprinkle in 2 packets gelatin and let it sit for 1 minute, letting the gelatin activate. Place saucepan over medium heat, whisking until gelatin dissolves. Bring to a light simmer, then remove from heat. Add the schnapps and rum. Let mixture come to room temperature.

4. Pour mixture on top of first layer. Refrigerate for 2 hours, or until firm.

5. Using a rubber spatula or butter knife, run it along the edge of the loaf pan to loosen the gelatin. Flip the pan onto a cutting board, releasing the gelatin whole. Slice gelatin into 5 slices.

6. Make 5 slices crosswise to cut squares. Refrigerate until serving.

EGGNOG

Love it or hate it—and I love it—eggnog is a Christmas classic. And this shot is definitely a fun spin on the spiked version of this holiday drink.

 Makes 12 shots

Ingredients

1½ cups (350 mL) eggnog

2 x ¼-ounce (7 g) packet Knox gelatin

½ cup (120 mL) rum or brandy

Whipped cream, for topping

Grated nutmeg, for topping

Instructions

1. Pour eggnog into a medium saucepan. Sprinkle in gelatin and let it sit for 1 minute, letting the gelatin activate. Place saucepan over medium heat, whisking until gelatin dissolves. Bring to a light simmer, then remove from heat. Add the rum or brandy.

2. Pour mixture into plastic shot glasses and refrigerate for 2 hours, or until firm.

3. Refrigerate until serving, Top with whipped cream and grated nutmeg before serving.

EGGNOG PUDDINGS

Creamy and easy to make, eggnog pudding is a perfect holiday treat. Add some booze and you have a party pleaser.

 Makes 12–14 large shots

Ingredients

3.4-ounce (96 g) box Jell-O vanilla instant pudding

¾ cup (240 mL) eggnog

½ cup (120 mL) Baileys Irish Cream

¼ cup (60 mL) brandy, rum, or bourbon

8-ounce (226 g) container extra creamy Cool Whip, thawed in refrigerator

12–14 wafer cookies

Whipped cream, for topping

Grated nutmeg, for topping

Instructions

1. Combine pudding and eggnog in a medium bowl with an electric mixer—it will be a little runny.

2. Fold the Baileys; brandy, rum, or bourbon; and Cool Whip into the pudding mixture until combined—don't overmix, but there should be no lumps.

3. Cover and place in freezer for 1 hour, or until firm but not frozen.

4. Spoon or pipe the pudding mixture into shot glasses. Refrigerate until serving. Add a cookie to each shot glass and top with whipped cream and grated nutmeg before serving.

CHRISTMAS TREES

A classic shot that's as easy to make as it is to pick up and enjoy. For a tropical Christmas twist, use lime-flavored Jell-O and Malibu Rum!

 Makes 15–20 shots

Ingredients

2 cups (475 mL) water

2 x 3-ounce (85 g) package green Jell-O

2 x ¼-ounce (7 g) packet Knox gelatin

2 cups (475 mL) Malibu Rum or flavored vodka of choice

15–20 maraschino cherries with stems, halved horizontally

Instructions

1. Add water and Jell-O to a medium saucepan and whisk to combine. Sprinkle in gelatin and let it sit for 1 minute, letting the gelatin activate. Place saucepan over medium heat, whisking until gelatin dissolves. Bring to a light simmer, then remove from heat. Add the rum or vodka.

2. Pour half of the mixture into a lightly greased 9 x 13-inch (23 x 33 cm) pan. Refrigerate for 30–60 minutes, or until sticky and slightly set but not firm.

3. Place cherry halves with stems in rows—with enough space to cut Christmas-tree shapes around them—on set layer.

4. Pour remaining mixture on top of the first layer. Reposition any cherries that move. Refrigerate for 2 hours, or until firm.

5. Carefully cut out the shots around the cherries with a Christmas tree–shaped cookie or fondant cutter and remove from pan. Refrigerate until serving.

CANDY CANES

For these shots, I came up with the idea to tilt the shot glasses so the layers form at an angle, like real candy canes. If you prefer to keep these all peppermint, replace the vanilla vodka with more peppermint schnapps.

 Makes 24–30 shots

Ingredients

3 cups (700 mL) water, divided

4 x ¼-ounce (7 g) packet Knox gelatin

6 tablespoons (75 g) sugar, divided

Red food coloring

1 cup (240 mL) peppermint schnapps

3-ounce (85 g) box red Jell-O

3 tablespoons (45 mL) sweetened condensed milk

1 cup (240 mL) vanilla-flavored vodka or peppermint schnapps

Whipped cream, for topping

24–30 mini candy canes, for serving (optional)

Instructions

1. To make red layer, pour 1 cup (240 mL) water into a medium saucepan. Sprinkle in 2 packets gelatin and let it sit for 1 minute, letting the gelatin activate. Place saucepan over medium heat, whisking until gelatin dissolves.

2. Add 3 tablespoons (37.5 g) sugar and whisk until it dissolves. Bring to a light simmer, then remove from heat. Add food coloring until desired color is achieved (I use 4–5 drops). Add schnapps and set aside, near the warm stove top to prevent hardening.

3. To make white layer, add 1 cup (240 mL) water and condensed milk to a medium saucepan and whisk to combine. Sprinkle in 2 packets gelatin and let it sit for 1 minute, letting the gelatin activate. Place saucepan over medium heat, whisking until gelatin dissolves.

4. Add 3 tablespoons (37.5 g) sugar and whisk until it dissolves. Bring to a light simmer, then remove from heat. Add the vodka or schnapps and set aside, near the warm stove top to prevent hardening.

5. Spoon 1 tablespoon (15 mL) of the red or white mixture into shot glasses and place glasses at a tilted angle in the cups of a muffin tin. Wait for layer to firm up, about 10 minutes, then spoon a tablespoon (15 mL) of the other color on top. Repeat this step until the glasses are full, without overflowing. Refrigerate for 2 hours, or until firm.

6. Refrigerate until serving. Top each shot with whipped cream and a mini candy cane, if desired, before serving.

TROPICAL WINTER

A step away from traditional Christmas colors, these shots are perfect for any winter party. I also love the extra flavor of the coconut flakes. And it looks like snow!

 Makes 24 shots

Ingredients

2 cups (475 mL) water

2 x 3-ounce (85 g) box berry blue Jell-O

2 x ¼-ounce (7 g) packet Knox gelatin

2 cups (475 mL) Malibu Rum

1 cup (93 g) coconut flakes

Instructions

1. Add water and Jell-O to a medium saucepan and whisk to combine. Sprinkle in gelatin and let it sit for 1 minute, letting the gelatin activate. Place saucepan over medium heat, whisking until gelatin dissolves. Bring to a light simmer, then remove from heat. Add the rum.

2. Pour mixture into a lightly greased 9 x 13-inch (23 x 33 cm) pan. Refrigerate for 2 hours, or until firm.

3. Carefully cut out shots with a mini square-shaped cookie or fondant cutter or a knife and remove from the pan. Refrigerate until serving. Sprinkle with coconut flakes before serving.

PEPPERMINT MOCHAS

Caffeinated shots are the perfect combination of my two favorite things: coffee and booze. The candy cane on the side is not only perfect for the holidays, but it can also be used to scoop the shot out of the glass!

 Makes 15 shots

Ingredients

1 cup (240 mL) coffee, warm

2 x ¼-ounce (7 g) packet Knox gelatin

¼ cup (50 g) sugar

1 cup (240 mL) Godiva Chocolate Liqueur or chocolate-flavored vodka

15 mini candy canes, for serving

Whipped cream, for topping

Instructions

1. Pour coffee into a medium saucepan. Sprinkle in gelatin and let it sit for 1 minute, letting the gelatin activate. Place saucepan over medium heat, whisking until gelatin dissolves.

2. Add sugar and whisk until it dissolves. Bring to a light simmer, then remove from heat. Add the chocolate liqueur or chocolate vodka. Pour mixture into shot glasses. Refrigerate for 2 hours, or until firm.

3. Refrigerate until serving. Add a mini candy cane to each shot and top with whipped cream before serving. (Do not stick the candy canes in while the gelatin is forming; they will dissolve.)

SUGAR COOKIES

Sugar cookies—another classic holiday treat! This shot really does taste like a sugar cookie and even looks a lot like raw cookie dough. Top these treats with any sprinkles you'd like.

 Makes 24 shots

Ingredients

1 cup (240 mL) milk

1 cup (240 mL) vanilla- or sweet cream–flavored coffee creamer

4 x ¼-ounce (7 g) Knox gelatin

1 cup (240 mL) Baileys Irish Crème

1 cup (240 mL) Dekuyper Buttershots or butterscotch schnapps

2 tablespoons (30 mL) imitation butter flavor (optional)

Sprinkles, for topping

Instructions

1. Add milk and vanilla- or sweet cream–flavored coffee creamer to a medium saucepan and whisk to combine. Sprinkle in gelatin and let it sit for 1 minute, letting the gelatin activate. Place saucepan over medium heat, whisking until gelatin dissolves. Bring to a light simmer, then remove from heat. Add Baileys, Buttershots or schnapps, and imitation butter flavor, if desired.

2. Pour mixture into a lightly greased 9 x 13-inch (23 x 33 cm) pan. Refrigerate for 2 hours, or until firm.

3. Carefully cut out shots with the rim of a shot glass or a mini round-shaped cookie or fondant cutter and remove from the pan. Refrigerate until serving. Top with sprinkles before serving.

CHAMPAGNE & STRAWBERRIES

This shot was one of the first I ever made for my blog. Champagne and strawberries are a classic combination, and they're perfect for any celebration. What makes this recipe really special is the whipped gelatin on top of the shots that resembles champagne foam.

 Makes 20 shots

Ingredients

1½ cups (350 mL) water

2 x 3-ounce (85 g) box island pineapple Jell-O

2½ cups (590 mL) champagne

1 cup (170 g) strawberries, sliced

Instructions

1. Pour water into a medium saucepan, bring to a boil, and lower heat to medium. Add the Jell-O and whisk until powder dissolves. Remove from heat. Refrigerate for 15 minutes.

2. Stir in champagne and refrigerate for another 30 minutes, or until gelatin has just slightly thickened.

3. Save ¾ cup (180 mL) of the mixture in the refrigerator to use later for the foam top.

4. Pour remaining mixture into plastic shot glasses, then drop a few sliced strawberries into each glass. Refrigerate for 2 hours, or until firm.

5. Refrigerate until serving. Before serving, whip the refrigerated ¾ cup (180 mL) mixture until it becomes white and fluffy and resembles foam. Spoon a small amount on top of each shot.

GRAPEFRUIT & PROSECCO

I love prosecco! What's the difference between prosecco and champagne? The biggest difference is that prosecco is Italian and champagne is French. Prosecco can also be a little bit sweeter, so it pairs well with tart and vibrant grapefruit.

 Makes 24–30 shots

Ingredients

2 cups (475 mL) ruby red grapefruit juice

4 x ¼-ounce (7 g) packet Knox gelatin

2 cups (475 mL) prosecco

Zest from 1 lemon, for topping

Instructions

1. Pour the grapefruit juice into a medium saucepan. Sprinkle in gelatin and let it sit for 1 minute, letting the gelatin activate. Place saucepan over medium heat, whisking until gelatin dissolves. Bring to a light simmer, then remove from heat. Add the prosecco, pouring slowly to prevent it from foaming excessively.

2. Pour the mixture into a lightly greased 9 x 13-inch (23 x 33 cm) pan. Refrigerate for 2 hours, or until firm.

3. Carefully cut out each shot with a mini square-shaped cookie or fondant cutter or a knife and remove from the pan. Refrigerate until serving. Top with citrus zest before serving.

PEACH & VANILLA CHAMPAGNE

I was looking for another way to make a New Year's Eve champagne shot extra tasty, when I came up with the idea of adding peach schnapps for some additional flavor and some aromatic vanilla for richness—think bites of peach cobbler chased with a sip of champagne.

 Makes 24–30 shots

Ingredients

1 bottle (750 mL) champagne

4 x ¼-ounce (7 g) packet Knox gelatin

¼ cup (50 g) sugar

Small splash vanilla extract

½ cup (120 mL) peach schnapps

Instructions

1. Pour 2 cups (475 mL) champagne in a medium saucepan. Sprinkle in gelatin and let it sit for 1 minute, letting the gelatin activate. Place saucepan over medium heat, whisking until gelatin dissolves.

2. Add the sugar and vanilla, and whisk until sugar dissolves. Bring to a light simmer, then remove from heat.

3. In a separate bowl, combine the remaining champagne with the peach schnapps. Stir in the warm champagne mixture.

4. Pour into a lightly greased 9 x 13-inch (23 x 33 cm) pan. Refrigerate for 2 hours, or until firm.

5. Carefully cut out shots with a mini star-shaped cookie or fondant cutter and remove from the pan. Refrigerate until serving.

Brunch

PINK FROSTED DONUTS

BACON BLOODY MARYS

TOMATO BLOODY MARYS

CINNAMON ROLLS

ESPRESSO MARTINIS

Special Occasions

CHOCOLATE HAZELNUT

BIRTHDAY CAKES

VODKA PICK-ME-UPS

COOKIE DOUGH PUDDING

JÄGER BOMBS

PEANUT BUTTER & JELLY

TRIPLE CHERRY COLA BOMBS

GUMMY BEARS

RAINBOW SQUARES

RAINBOW PINWHEELS

PINK FROSTED DONUTS

These shots are adorable and taste just like donuts. This recipe does require two mini donut molds to achieve the donut shape, but for a brunch party, they are so worth it.

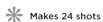 Makes 24 shots

Ingredients

1 cup (240 mL) water, divided

½ cup (120 mL) sweetened condensed milk, divided

Red or pink food coloring

2 x ¼-ounce (7 g) Knox gelatin, divided

1 cup (240 mL) cake- or donut-flavored vodka, divided

2 tablespoons (11 g) cocoa powder or 2 tablespoons (56 g) hot chocolate mix

Yellow food coloring

Sprinkles, for topping

Instructions

1. To make the pink frosting layer, add ½ cup (120 mL) water and ¼ cup (60 mL) sweetened condensed milk to a small saucepan and whisk to combine. Add red or pink food coloring until you reach desired color for pink frosting (I use 2–3 drops).

2. Sprinkle in 1 packet gelatin and let it sit for 1 minute, letting the gelatin activate. Place saucepan over medium heat, whisking until gelatin dissolves. Bring to a light simmer, then remove from heat. Add ½ cup (120 mL) vodka.

3. Pour mixture into lightly greased mini donut molds, filling them halfway. Refrigerate the molds for 30–60 minutes, or until sticky and slightly set but not firm.

4. To make the donut layer, add ½ cup (120 mL) water and ¼ cup (60 mL) sweetened condensed milk to a small saucepan and whisk to combine. Whisk in cocoa powder or hot chocolate mix. Add yellow food coloring until you reach desired "donut" color (I use 5–7 drops).

5. Sprinkle in 1 packet gelatin and let it sit for 1 minute, letting the gelatin activate. Place saucepan over medium heat, whisking until gelatin dissolves. Bring to a light simmer, then remove from heat. Add ½ cup (120 mL) vodka. Let mixture come to room temperature.

6. Pour mixture on top of pink layer in the molds. Refrigerate for 2 hours, or until firm.

7. Carefully remove shots from the molds— they should slide out somewhat easily if set properly. Refrigerate until serving. Top with sprinkles before serving.

BACON BLOODY MARYS

Anything with bacon is a winner in my book (no pun intended). I don't do a lot of savory shots, but these are delicious. For an extra kick, spice these up with pepper- or sriracha-flavored vodka.

 Makes 24 shots

Ingredients

2 cups (475 ml) Bloody Mary mix of choice

4 x ¼-ounce (7 g) Knox gelatin

2 cups (475 mL) vodka flavor of choice

5–10 slices cooked, crispy bacon, crumbled, for topping

Spanish olives, halved, for topping (optional)

Instructions

1. Pour Bloody Mary mix into a medium saucepan. Sprinkle in gelatin and let it sit for 1 minute, letting the gelatin activate. Place saucepan over medium heat, whisking until gelatin dissolves. Bring to a light simmer, then remove from heat. Add the vodka.

2. Pour mixture into a lightly greased 9 x 13-inch (23 x 33 cm) pan. Refrigerate for 2 hours, or until firm.

3. Carefully cut out shots with a mini square-shaped cookie or fondant cutter or a knife and remove from pan. Refrigerate until serving. Top with bacon and olives, if desired, before serving.

TOMATO BLOODY MARYS

These shots are so easy to eat. Simply pop the tomato wedge in your mouth and that's it. You can add any Bloody Mary topping you like to the cocktail stick: bacon, celery, olives, pickles...be creative!

 Makes 20 shots

Ingredients

5 campari tomatoes

½ cup (120 mL) Bloody Mary mix of choice

¼-ounce (7 g) packet Knox gelatin

½ cup (120 mL) vodka flavor of choice

Old Bay Seasoning, to taste

20 cocktail sticks

20 Spanish olives, for serving

Instructions

1. Halve campari tomatoes horizontally and gently hollow them out with a melon baller or spoon. Gently dry the insides with a paper towel. Line up halves on a baking sheet or place in a muffin tin so they are secure and upright, and set aside.

2. Pour Bloody Mary mix into a small saucepan. Sprinkle in gelatin and let it sit for 1 minute, letting the gelatin activate. Place saucepan over medium heat, whisking until gelatin dissolves. Bring to a light simmer, then remove from heat. Add the vodka.

3. Pour mixture into spouted bowl or measuring cup, then carefully pour it into tomato halves. Refrigerate for 2 hours, or until firm.

4. Slice tomato halves in half and dip them in Old Bay Seasoning. Refrigerate until serving. Place each shot onto a cocktail stick with a Spanish olive and any topping you like before serving.

CINNAMON ROLLS

This shot really does taste just like your favorite guilty breakfast pleasure. For added flavor, you can even use cinnamon roll–flavored vodka instead of butterscotch schnapps.

 Makes 15–24 shots

Ingredients

½ cup (120 mL) Baileys Irish Cream

½ cup (120 mL) butterscotch schnapps

2 x ¼-ounce (7 g) packet Knox gelatin

1–2 tablespoons (15–30 mL) sweetened condensed milk

1 teaspoon (5 mL) cinnamon or cocoa powder

½ cup (120 mL) cinnamon schnapps

½ cup (120 mL) water

Small tube white icing

Instructions

1. Add Baileys and butterscotch schnapps to a medium saucepan and whisk to combine. Sprinkle in gelatin and let it sit for 1 minute, letting the gelatin activate. Place saucepan over medium heat, whisking until gelatin dissolves. Add sweetened condensed milk—use 2 tablespoons (30 mL) if you want it really sweet. Whisk again.

2. Add the cinnamon or cocoa powder—this will make the mixture a darker brown color. Strain out any clumps of cocoa or cinnamon you can't incorporate. Add cinnamon schnapps and water.

3. Pour mixture into a lightly greased 9 x 13-inch (23 x 33 cm) pan. Refrigerate for 2 hours, or until firm.

4. Carefully cut out shots with the rim of a shot glass or a mini round-shaped cookie or fondant cutter and remove from the pan. Refrigerate until serving. Top with swirls of white icing before serving.

ESPRESSO MARTINIS

These shots are a perfect combination of strong coffee and sweet liqueur. Pick one up and enjoy the buzz.

✳ Makes 24 shots

Ingredients

1 cup (240 mL) coffee, cold

4 x ¼-ounce (7 g) packet Knox gelatin, divided

1 cup (240 mL) espresso-flavored vodka

1 cup (240 mL) water

4 tablespoons (60 mL) sweetened condensed milk

1 cup (240 mL) Baileys Irish Cream

24 coffee beans, whole, for topping

Instructions

1. To make the brown layer, pour coffee into a medium saucepan. Sprinkle in 2 packets gelatin and let it sit for 1 minute, letting the gelatin activate. Place saucepan over medium heat, whisking until gelatin dissolves. Bring to a light simmer, then remove from heat. Add the vodka.

2. Pour mixture into a lightly greased 9 x 13-inch (23 x 33 cm) pan. Refrigerate for 30–60 minutes, or until sticky and slightly set but not firm.

3. To make the white layer, add water and sweetened condensed milk to a medium saucepan and whisk to combine. Sprinkle in 2 packets gelatin and let it sit for 1 minute, letting the gelatin activate. Place saucepan over medium heat, whisking until gelatin dissolves. Bring to a light simmer, then remove from heat. Add the Baileys. Let mixture come to room temperature.

4. Pour mixture on top of coffee layer. Refrigerate for 2 hours, or until firm.

5. Carefully cut out shots with a mini square-shaped cookie or fondant cutter or a knife and remove from pan. Refrigerate until serving. Top each one with a coffee bean before serving.

CHOCOLATE HAZELNUT

When I discovered that mixing Frangelico and butterscotch schnapps tastes just like Nutella, I knew I had to make a shot right away. If you're a Nutella lover, too, these are for you!

 Makes 32–40 shots

Ingredients

1 cup (240 mL) water

3 heaping tablespoons (84 g) hot chocolate mix

2 x ¼ ounce (7 g) packet Knox gelatin

½ cup (120 mL) Frangelico

½ cup (120 mL) butterscotch schnapps

Zest from 1 orange or lemon, for topping

Instructions

1. Add water and hot chocolate mix to a medium saucepan and whisk to combine. Sprinkle in gelatin and let it sit for 1 minute, letting the gelatin activate. Place saucepan over medium heat, whisking until gelatin dissolves. Bring to a light simmer, then remove from heat. Add Frangelico and butterscotch schnapps.

2. Pour mixture into a lightly greased 7½ x 3½-inch (19 x 9 cm) loaf pan. Refrigerate for 2 hours, or until firm.

3. Using a rubber spatula or butter knife, run it along the edge of the loaf pan to loosen the gelatin. Flip the pan onto a cutting board, releasing the gelatin whole. Slice gelatin as if you were slicing bread, into 8 slices.

4. Make 4–5 vertical slices to cut squares. Refrigerate until serving. Top each shot with lemon or orange zest before serving.

BIRTHDAY CAKES

I really, really love these shots. You can change the color of the frosting to anything you like. The vanilla butter and nut flavoring really makes them special and can be found at most large grocery stores in the same aisle as vanilla extract.

 Makes 20–24 shots

Ingredients

4 cups (950 ml) water

6 tablespoons (90 mL) sweetened condensed milk, divided

2 tablespoons (30 mL) vanilla butter and nut flavoring

6 x ¼ ounce (7 g) Knox gelatin, divided

2 cups (240 mL) cake-flavored vodka

20–24 maraschino cherries with stems, halved horizontally

Pink food coloring

Sprinkles, for topping

Instructions

1. For the first cake layer, add 1 cup (240 mL) water and 2 tablespoons (30 mL) condensed milk to a medium saucepan and whisk to combine. Add 1 tablespoon (15 mL) vanilla butter and nut flavoring and whisk again. Sprinkle in 2 packets gelatin and let sit for 1 minute, letting gelatin activate. Place saucepan over medium heat, whisking until gelatin is dissolved. Bring to a light simmer, then remove from heat. Add the vodka.

2. Pour mixture into a lightly greased 9 x 13-inch (23 x 33 cm) pan. Refrigerate for 30–60 minutes, or until sticky and slightly set but not firm. Place cherry halves with stems in rows—with enough space to cut triangles around them—on set layer.

3. For the second layer, repeat steps 1–2, letting mixture come to room temperature before pouring into pan. Reposition any cherries that move.

4. For the pink frosting layer, add 1 cup (240 mL) water and 2 tablespoons (30 mL) condensed milk to a medium saucepan and whisk to combine. Add pink food coloring until desired color is achieved (I use 10 drops). Sprinkle in 2 packets gelatin and let it sit for 1 minute, letting the gelatin activate. Place saucepan over medium heat, whisking until gelatin dissolves. Bring to a light simmer, then remove from heat. Add 1 cup (240 mL) water. Let mixture come to room temperature.

5. Pour mixture on top of cake layers, until you have desired thickness. Refrigerate for 2 hours, or until firm.

6. Carefully cut out shots around the cherries with a mini triangle-shaped cookie or fondant cutter and remove from pan. Refrigerate until serving. Top with sprinkles before serving.

VODKA PICK-ME-UPS

Need a pick-me-up? These are one of my most famous shots, and they will make you and everyone else the life of the party! You can use either regular or sugar-free Red Bull.

 Makes 24 shots

Ingredients

1½ cups (350 mL) Red Bull (about 1 x 12-ounce, 355 mL, can)

1½ x ¼-ounce (7 g) packet Knox gelatin

½ cup (120 mL) vodka flavor of choice

24 maraschino cherries with stems, halved horizontally

Instructions

1. Pour Red Bull into a medium saucepan. Sprinkle in gelatin and let it sit for 1 minute, letting the gelatin activate. Place saucepan over medium heat, whisking until gelatin dissolves. Bring to a light simmer, then remove from heat. Add the vodka.

2. Pour half of the mixture into a lightly greased 9 x 13-inch (23 x 33 cm) pan. Refrigerate for 30–60 minutes, or until sticky and slightly set but not firm. Let remaining mixture come to room temperature.

3. Place cherry halves with stems in rows—with enough space to cut squares around them—on the set layer. Pour the remaining mixture on top of the first layer. Reposition any cherries that move. Refrigerate for 2 hours, or until firm.

4. Carefully cut out shots around the cherries with a mini square-shaped cookie or fondant cutter or a knife and remove from pan. Refrigerate until serving.

COOKIE DOUGH PUDDING

These pudding shots are buttery, brown sugary, chocolaty, and boozy. Use a good-quality vodka, such as Pinnacle cookie dough or vanilla. You can find the imitation butter flavor next to vanilla extract in most grocery stores.

 Makes 18 shots

Ingredients

3.4-ounce (96 g) box Jello-O instant vanilla or French vanilla pudding

¾ cup (180 mL) milk

¼ cup (60 mL) butterscotch schnapps

½ cup (120 mL) vanilla- or cookie dough–flavored vodka

8-ounce (226 g) container Cool Whip, thawed in refrigerator

2 tablespoons (30 mL) imitation butter flavor

¾ cup (131 g) mini chocolate chips, plus extra for topping

¾ cup (135 g) brown sugar

Whipped cream, for topping

Instructions

1. Combine pudding and milk with an electric mixer in a large bowls—it will be semi-thick.

2. Fold the schnapps, vodka, and Cool Whip into the pudding mixture until combined—don't overmix, but there should be no lumps. Fold in imitation butter flavor, chocolate chips, and brown sugar. Place in freezer for 1 hour, or until firm but not frozen.

3. Spoon or pipe pudding mixture into plastic shot glasses. Refrigerate until serving. Top each shot with whipped cream and chocolate chips before serving.

JÄGER BOMBS

Jäger bombs were a popular drink when I was in college. The sweetness of the Red Bull in this recipe takes over, so you can hardly taste the strong licorice flavor of the Jägermeister.

 Makes 20 shots

Ingredients

4 cups (950 mL) Red Bull (about 2 x 16-ounce, or 473 mL, can), divided

5 x ¼-ounce (7 g) packet Knox gelatin, divided

1 cup (240 mL) Jägermeister, divided

Instructions

1. Pour 2 cups (475 mL) Red Bull into a medium saucepan. Sprinkle in 4 packets gelatin and let it sit for 1 minute, letting the gelatin activate. Place saucepan over medium heat, whisking until gelatin dissolves. Bring to a light simmer, then remove from heat. Add remaining 2 cups (475 mL) Red Bull.

2. Pour mixture into a lightly greased 9 x 13-inch (23 x 33 cm) pan. Refrigerate for 2 hours, or until firm.

3. Carefully cut out gelatin with an extra-mini square-shaped cookie or fondant cutter to create cavities for the Jägermeister mixture, discarding the removed gelatin—leave enough room to cut out larger squares around the cavities. Place pan back in refrigerator.

4. Pour ½ cup (120 mL) Jägermeister into a small saucepan. Sprinkle in remaining packet gelatin and let it sit for 1 minute, letting the gelatin activate. Place saucepan over medium heat, whisking until gelatin dissolves. Bring to a light simmer, then remove from heat. Add remaining ½ cup (120 mL) Jägermeister. Let mixture come to room temperature.

5. Using a dropper or small spoon, carefully pour the mixture into the cavities—don't worry if they overflow a little. Refrigerate for 2 hours, or until firm.

6. Carefully cut out shots with a mini square-shaped cookie or fondant cutter or a knife and remove from pan. Refrigerate until serving.

PEANUT BUTTER & JELLY

These shots are simple and classic, just like the sandwich...except for the booze in them, of course. And the Jell-O!

 Makes 32–40 shots

Ingredients

1½ cups (360 mL) water, divided

4 tablespoons (64 g) creamy peanut butter

¼ cup (60 mL) sweetened condensed milk

2½ x ¼-ounce (7 g) packet Knox gelatin, divided

1½ cups (360 mL) marshmallow-flavored vodka, divided

3-ounce (85 g) box grape Jell-O

Instructions

1. To make peanut butter layer, add ¾ cup (180 mL) water, peanut butter, and sweetened condensed milk to a medium saucepan and whisk to combine. Sprinkle in 2 packets gelatin and let it sit for 1 minute, letting the gelatin activate. Place saucepan over medium heat, whisking until gelatin dissolves. Bring to a light simmer, then remove from heat. Add ¾ cup (180 mL) vodka.

2. Pour mixture into a lightly greased 7½ x 3½-inch (19 x 9-cm) loaf pan. Refrigerate for 30–60 minutes, or until sticky and slightly set but not firm.

3. To make jelly layer, add ¾ cup (180 mL) water and Jell-O to a medium saucepan and whisk to combine. Sprinkle in ½ packet gelatin and let it sit for 1 minute, letting the gelatin activate. Place saucepan over medium heat, whisking until gelatin dissolves. Bring to a light simmer, then remove from heat. Add remaining ¾ cup (180 mL) vodka. Let mixture come to room temperature.

4. Pour mixture on top of peanut butter layer. Refrigerate for 2 hours, or until firm.

5. Using a rubber spatula or butter knife, run it along the edge of the loaf pan to loosen the gelatin. Flip the pan onto a cutting board, releasing the gelatin whole. Slice gelatin as if you were slicing bread, into 8 slices.

6. Make 4–5 vertical slices to cut squares. Refrigerate until serving.

TRIPLE CHERRY COLA BOMBS

Cherries soaked in cherry vodka surrounded by Cherry Coke that's also been infused with cherry vodka? Triple BOOM!

 Makes 15–20 shots

Ingredients

15–20 maraschino cherries with stems

2 cups (480 mL) cherry-flavored vodka, divided

2 cups (480 mL) Cherry Coke, divided

4 x ¼-ounce (7 g) packet Knox gelatin, divided

Instructions

1. Place maraschino cherries in 1 cup (240 mL) vodka and let soak for at least 1 hour—you can also soak them overnight.

2. Pour 1 cup (240 mL) Cherry Coke into a medium saucepan. Sprinkle in 2 packets gelatin and let it sit for 1 minute, letting the gelatin activate. Place saucepan over medium heat, whisking until gelatin dissolves. Bring to a light simmer, then remove from heat. Add 1 cup (240 mL) vodka.

3. Pour mixture into a lightly greased 9 x 13-inch (23 x 33 cm) pan. Refrigerate for 30–60 minutes, or until sticky and slightly set but not firm.

4. Remove maraschino cherries from vodka and set vodka aside. Halve the cherries horizontally.

5. Repeat step 2 but with the vodka that the cherries were soaking in. Let mixture come to room temperature. Pour mixture on top of the first layer. Place cherry halves with stems in rows—with enough space to cut squares around them—in the mixture. Refrigerate for at least 2 hours, or until firm.

6. Carefully cut out shots around the cherries with a mini square-shaped cookie or fondant cutter or a knife and remove from pan. Refrigerate until serving.

GUMMY BEARS

Who doesn't love gummy bears? I would suggest using Haribo brand gummy bears, as they hold their shape when making these shots.

 Makes 15 shots

Ingredients

2 cups (480 mL) water, divided

2 cups (400 g) sugar, divided

4 x ¼-ounce (7 g) packet Knox gelatin, divided

2 cups (480 mL) gummy bear–flavored vodka, divided

15 gummy bears, chilled

Instructions

1. Add 1 cup (240 mL) water and 1 cup (200 g) sugar to a medium saucepan and whisk to combine. Sprinkle in 2 packets gelatin and let it sit for 1 minute, letting the gelatin activate. Place saucepan over medium heat, whisking until sugar and gelatin are dissolved. Bring to a light simmer, then remove from heat. Add 1 cup (240 mL) vodka.

2. Pour into a lightly greased 9 x 13-inch (23 x 33 cm) pan. Refrigerate 30–60 minutes, or until sticky and slightly set but not firm.

3. Repeat step 1. Let mixture come to room temperature.

4. Place gummy bears in rows—with enough space to cut squares around them—into set layer in pan, leaving their heads sticking out of the gelatin. Pour mixture on top of first layer and gummies. Refrigerate for 2 hours, or until firm.

5. Carefully cut out shots around gummy bears with a mini square-shaped cookie or fondant cutter or a knife and remove from pan. Refrigerate until serving.

RAINBOW SQUARES

For this recipe, I've mixed and matched some basic colors to achieve a gorgeous spectrum of boozy fun. You'll have some leftover red and blue gelatin, so if you don't want it to go to waste, try adding a purple layer or make single, solid-colored shots.

 Makes 24 shots

Ingredients

3 cups (720 mL) water, divided

3-ounce (85 g) box red Jell-O

3 x ¼-ounce (7 g) packet Knox gelatin, divided

3 cups (720 mL) flavored vodka of choice, divided

3-ounce (85 g) box yellow Jell-O

3-ounce (85 g) box blue Jell-O

Instructions

1. To make the red layer, add 1 cup (240 mL) water and red Jell-O to a medium saucepan and whisk to combine. Sprinkle in 1 packet gelatin and let it sit for 1 minute, letting the gelatin activate. Place saucepan over medium heat, whisking until gelatin dissolves. Bring to a light simmer, then remove from heat. Add 1 cup (240 mL) vodka.

2. Pour 1 cup (240 mL) of mixture into a lightly greased 9 x 13-inch (23 x 33 cm) pan. Refrigerate for 30–60 minutes, or until sticky and slightly set but not firm. Set aside remaining 1 cup (240 mL) mixture by warm stove top so it doesn't cool off.

3. To make the yellow layer, repeat step 1 with yellow Jell-O. Let mixture come to room temperature.

4. Pour 1½ cups (350 mL) of mixture on top of red layer. Refrigerate for 30–60 minutes, or until yellow layer is sticky and slightly set but not firm. Set aside remaining ½ cup (120 mL) mixture near warm stove top, with remaining red mixture.

5. To make the blue layer, repeat step 1 with blue Jell-O. Let mixture come to room temperature.

6. Combine ½ cup (120 mL) blue mixture with remaining ½ cup (120 mL) yellow mixture to make 1 cup (240 mL) green mixture.

7. Pour green mixture on top of yellow layer in pan. Set aside remaining 1½ cups (350 mL) of blue mixture near stove top. Refrigerate for 30–60 minutes, or until green layer is sticky and slightly set but not firm.

8. Pour 1 cup (240 mL) of remaining blue mixture on top of green layer in pan. Refrigerate for 2 hours, or until blue layer is firm.

9. Carefully cut out shots with a mini square-shaped cookie or fondant cutter or a knife and remove from pan. Refrigerate until serving.

RAINBOW PINWHEELS

How cool are these? I've seen these floating around the Internet and wondered if I could add booze to them. Well guess what? You can! Here are a few tips: Use brand new, fresh marshmallows; don't overheat the Jell-O or marshmallows; and make sure your measurements are precise.

 Makes 12 shots

Ingredients

3-ounce (85 g) box Jell-O color/flavor of choice

½ cup (120 mL) whipped cream–flavored vodka or vodka flavor of choice

1 cup (50 g) fresh miniature marshmallows

Instructions

1. Add the Jell-O and vodka to a medium microwaveable bowl. Microwave for 40 seconds—just enough to dissolve the gelatin but not cook out the booze.

2. Immediately add the marshmallows to the heated mixture. Microwave for another 20 seconds—do not overheat the marshmallows.

3. Immediately whisk the marshmallows right until they dissolve—this should take 30 seconds maximum.

4. Pour the mixture into a lightly greased 9 x 9-inch (23 x 23 cm) square cake pan. Refrigerate for 1 hour.

5. Run a rubber spatula or a butter knife around the edge of the pan to loosen the gelatin. Carefully peel up one end of the gelatin and slowly roll it toward the other end. Remove the roll from the pan, then slice ½–1-inch-wide (1.25–2.5 cm) rolls. Refrigerate until serving.

DEDICATION

This cookbook is dedicated to my husband, Nick. Thank you for always being my biggest fan. I don't think there is a single person (including friends and strangers) that you haven't told about my blog and this cookbook. Tears well up in my eyes when I think about how genuinely proud of me you always are. I couldn't have done this without you. You are my Jelly Shot King and ruler of my heart always.

ACKNOWLEDGMENTS

Special thanks to my mom, who helped watch my little man so his mommy could write a cookbook, and my editor, Jeannine Dillon, who was fun enough to envision all of this and help me make it happen.

Photo © Michelle's Mom

ABOUT THE AUTHOR

Michelle Cordero is the woman behind the popular food and lifestyle blog That's So Michelle. Dubbed the "Jello Shot Queen," Michelle's boozy party creations have been featured in *Bon Appétit, Cosmopolitan, Glamour, Buzzfeed, Country Living, Redbook,* and more! She has close to twelve thousand followers on Pinterest and over five thousand followers on Facebook.

During the day, Michelle works in PR for a think tank in Washington, DC. She was formerly a reporter and has appeared on Fox News and MSNBC.

She lives in Virginia with her husband, Nick, and their son. You can learn more about Michelle at www.thatssomichelle.com.